Free
Shakespeare

THE APPLAUSE SHAKESPEARE LIBRARY

A MIDSUMMER NIGHT'S DREAM
prepared by John Russell Brown, John Hirsch, and Leslie
Thompson

KING LEAR
edited by John Russell Brown

MACBETH
prepared by R. A. Foakes and John Russell Brown

THE TEMPEST
edited by John Russell Brown

JULIUS CAESAR
prepared by Maurice Charney and Stuart Vaughan

SHAKESCENES: SHAKESPEARE FOR TWO
edited by John Russell Brown

SHAKESPEARE'S PLAYS IN PERFORMANCE
John Russell Brown

ACTING WITH SHAKESPEARE: THE COMEDIES
Janet Suzman

THE ACTOR AND THE TEXT
Cicely Berry

**SOLILOQUY: THE SHAKESPEARE MONOLOGUES
(MEN)**
edited by Michael Earley and Philippa Keil

**SOLILOQUY: THE SHAKESPEARE MONOLOGUES
(WOMEN)**
edited by Michael Earley and Philippa Keil

**THE COMPLEAT WORKS OF WLLM SHKSPR
(ABRIDGED)**
Jess Borgeson, Adam Long, and Daniel Singer

Free Shakespeare

NEW AND EXPANDED EDITION
JOHN RUSSELL BROWN

APPLAUSE
NEW YORK • LONDON

Free Shakespeare
by John Russell Brown
© John Russell Brown 1974, 1997
ISBN 1-55783-283-8

Library of Congress Cataloging-in-Publication Data

LC Catalog # 97-71439

British Library Cataloging-in-Publication Data
A catalogue record of this book is available from the British Library.

APPLAUSE BOOKS

211 West 71st Street
New York, NY 10023
Phone (212) 496-7511
Fax: (212) 721-2856

A&C BLACK

Howard Road, Eaton Socon
Huntington, Cambs PE19 3EZ
Phone 0171-242 0946
Fax 0171-831 8478

First Applause Printing, 1997

Contents

Acknowledgements

The ideas expressed in this book have derived from my experience as a theatre director, and as a member of the audience for many productions. They have been developed through contact with many people. Invitations to give the Annual Lecture in Drama at the University of Toronto, the Annual Public Lecture of the Society for Theatre Research, London, and the Sidney Jones Lectures at the University of Liverpool gave me both stimulus and criticism. Seminars at the Universities of Birmingham and Sussex, and at Stratford Ontario and Stratford Connecticut, provided questions, suggestions and further exploration. I am most grateful for all these opportunities and, while the faults of my book are my own responsibility, I am very conscious of how much I owe to others in tackling this work.

I have drawn on earlier forms of my argument that appeared in various periodicals: 'The Theatrical Element of Shakespeare Criticism', *Reinterpretations of Elizabethan Drama*, ed. N. Rabkin (New York, 1969); 'Free Shakespeare', *Shakespeare Survey*, 24 (1971); 'Settings for Shakespeare', *Interscaena '71*, i (1971); 'Originality in Shakespeare Production', *Theatre Notebook*, xxvi (1972) and 'Speaking Shakespeare's Lines', *Shakespeare Jahrbuch* (1972).

I

Shakespeare Today

As we learn more about the history of a work of art and grow more capable of analysing its various parts and aspects, so direct experience becomes more rare. It is easier to recognize the fitness of a description than to respond for ourselves. Our minds are kept busy dealing with the information that is fed to us so that, while we have become capable of a fuller recognition, we seem to have less opportunity for achieving this. The ability to understand the context and construction of a work of art, and the pleasures of exercising this intellectual resource, cannot guarantee an experience which reaches further into ourselves. Frequently they serve to protect us against shock and to inhibit the leap of individual imaginative belief.

In a picture gallery a class of children will stand fidgeting while their teacher explains; if they look at the painting it is to verify the information. A new kind of reader is being trained in schools and colleges, who reaches for a collection of criticisms – a 'Handbook', 'Casebook' or 'Readers' Guide' – at the same time as he takes down a volume of poems from the shelves: so he will find not one viewpoint but many, and he will be encouraged to engage in the critical debate for himself. In a theatre we purchase large and illustrated programmes which tell the story of the play, explain its themes, show the actors rehearsing and quote the praises of critics. Shakespeare's plays are presented in ever new productions, each one of which will emphasize one particular interpretation and display the talents of its director and actors. The devoted Shakespearian will seek out many different productions and slowly build up a complex memory-system which will provide him with a multiple response for each favourite play; but by this time he may well be devoted to the pursuit and not to the quarry.

In such a well-informed and various world, the survival of individual, open, imaginative and creative response poses yet another major problem. How can we avoid the secondary response, see the goods and not the package, maintain a crucial ignorance, but not a *naïveté*? We have a virtually free access to books of learning and have been encouraged since youth to pass examinations, so that it now seems natural to have an informed opinion on any subject worth the study. Yet we know that deepest experiences are not examinable, and that verbalization stops short of accounting for those moments when we have recognized truth and moved outwards towards the encompassing of its new experience. Somehow we must defend our own creative response and strengthen it. This will not mean burning our books or trying to reconstruct primitive conditions. Rather we must examine the processing which art receives today, and our own consumption of it. We must use new skills responsibly, without expecting too much from them.

*   *   *

Our response to Shakespeare poses these difficulties in extreme form. He inherited beliefs and expertise we no longer possess. He responded to social and political realities that can only be reconstructed painstakingly by analysis and description. He wrote plays for a kind of theatre that no longer exists and cannot be reconstructed. He wrote texts for actors to explore and recreate rather than for the solitary reader, and he was aware of an audience that shared its pleasures. He has left no direct testimony of his intentions and we know only a little more than nothing about his private life. Obviously we can use many aids to understanding and consequently the books written about his plays and the productions of them in theatres throughout the world are unequalled in quantity and growing frequency. While there is no doubt that Shakespeare has survived through all the changes of time, that only increases the danger that his plays will be processed more completely. By making him our own, we may have lost what he can, uniquely, offer.

The task of this present book is an examination of the work of Shakespearian scholars, critics, teachers, directors and actors, and of the involvement of each reader and member of audience. The conditions under which we encounter Shakespeare cannot be changed easily, but a recognition of their effects upon us may make us able to defend ourselves against certain prejudices and enable us to suit response to occasion and opportunity. I shall propose particular experiments that could be undertaken by both readers and theatre producers. These run counter to much commercial and educational practice, but my experience shows that they can work in small scale and can therefore provide the beginnings of change.

Three main themes develop in the course of this book, all concerned with our response to Shakespeare. The most basic concern is to inquire how to read the plays imaginatively: what can we do to ensure an active encounter in which Shakespeare's words are the one fixed element in an image of our own lives (and even they are changing in appearance and effect all the time)? I want to argue that we must free the plays from one-sided interpretations, however subtle or well-informed, or however numerous, and for the time being forget the convenience and reassurance of nice definitions. On the other hand, I do not think that seeing the usual kinds of Shakespeare productions will help the reader to advance much further. Rather, he must seek interplay with the plays, explorations of an everchanging human image. This poses problems as considerable for the ordinary reader as for the teacher of a class in school, college or university: it requires an open mind and imaginative reach.

My most obvious theme is theatrical: I want to propose an alternative way of performing the plays, one that goes against almost all accepted conditions of production. Indeed I shall argue that the very concept of a 'production' confines a basic dramatic excitement that is inherent in the texts. For this part of my argument I will consider how plays were staged in Shakespeare's own time, but this does not mean that I want to see museum productions that seek to reconstruct the past. The kind of performances that I seek are so far from present-day theatre practice, except in rehearsals, that the Elizabethan theatre provides closer analogies: it also helps me to demonstrate that in other ages the procedures I suggest were not considered unprofessional or impossibly difficult. While any way of performing Shakespeare needs a full professional engagement in order to respond to the texts with sufficient expertise, it may well be true that a basically new approach can best start in amateur or student theatre groups, and so what I have to say may seem more immediately applicable to these than to our subsidized theatres. A 'free' performance would not be expensive in terms of modern production costs but at the outset its actors must be able to fail and still continue to work.

My third theme is one that is implicit only. I see no absolute division between my response to Shakespeare when I read the plays at home, teach them in a class room, see them in performance, or work on them in the theatre. I think that all these encounters can be mutually supporting, each providing special experiences and each helping the others to remain free and open to whatever the plays can give. In this book my attention moves between all these responses to Shakespeare, and that in itself is part of my subject, the freeing of Shakespeare's plays from restrictive presuppositions and the limitations of inherited procedures.

2

Directors and Scholars: the intellectual response

There is no question of Shakespeare's continual hold over men's imaginations. In the theatre, as Peter Brook wrote in *The Empty Space* (1968):

> in the second half of the twentieth century in England . . .we are faced with the infuriating fact that Shakespeare is still our model.
> (p. 95)

But our response is different from that of other ages. Brook continued by saying that

> our work on Shakespeare production is always to make the plays 'modern', because it is only when the audience comes into direct contact with the plays' themes that time and conventions vanish.

The significant word here is 'themes': we have used Shakespeare for our own intellectual purposes.

Other ages were quick to acknowledge that they had modernized the plays. Texts have been restyled, rewritten, translated into other forms, and recreated; and so the plays have been enjoyed by every generation. They have been adapted to new theatres, new actors and new audiences. In the Restoration, poets were proud to say that they had made Shakespeare 'fit', purging the text of the barbarities of a less civilized, less polished age. The eighteenth-century and romantic theatres, in their different ways, gave most attention to the major characters. Neglecting the comedies, they re-created Richard III, Macbeth and Lady Macbeth, Othello and Iago, as emotional, passionate and intense heroes. A few star actors ruled the stage, and from Shakespeare's text they cut what they could not use and added what they fancied. They pounced on single lines with which they could make 'points', electrically charged transitions between hope and despair, or between suffering and cruelty Meanwhile the physical form of the theatre was changing so that picturesque scenery began to be elaborated: crowd movements, gunsmoke, antiquarian interior scenes or mountains in the far-off distance, all began to make their own effects, sometimes without a word of Shakespeare's text to accompany them, or even to provide a point of departure. Then, around 1880, Henry Irving accentuated the melodramatic elements in the plays, and at the same time he and others began to seek original interpretations of Shakespeare's characters, based on sentimental and psychological study of the *minutiae* of the text, and also on the technical accomplishments and personality of the leading actor. This was the Shakespeare of Victorian novelists and moralists, of Ibsen and Andrew Bradley. The installation of electric light in the theatres intensified dramatic shock and contrast, and sharpened the focus on the star performer who was now illuminated with a follow-spot. More of Shakespeare's text was restored, actors took time for careful effects and scenery grew more complicated and picturesque. Productions were so slow that *Hamlet* – still without Fortinbras, but with Claudius's prayer-scene partially restored for the first time for centuries – ran for over five hours on a first night.

We readily believe that other ages refashioned Shakespeare in their own images. It is a familiar story, given credence by illustrations taken from old books and albums, and later by photographs. The immobility and defiance in the stances of these elderly actors, and the incongruity of their dress, facial expressions and backgrounds, make an effect on us at once. They mark the deviation from what we are accustomed to expect, and also from our knowledge of Elizabethan portraits and other artefacts. Old stage photographs are so different from those of our own theatre, that in them we can see most clearly how Shakespeare's plays have changed even in this present century, and how they are still changing as we continue to modernize. The well-spaced elegance and insistent stylishness that can be seen in the illustrations of Granville-Barker's Savoy productions of the years immediately before the First World War remind us quickly that the scholar-director (whose good sense is still acclaimed by both scholars and directors) must have shown Shakespeare's plays in a cold, meticulous light. In this theatre, Shakespeare was arty, clear, quick and well-organized. *Twelfth Night* would be set entirely in black and white, the only bright colour being the red wig of Olivia who was decked out to look like Queen Elizabeth I. Even photographs from the nineteen-fifties, showing productions by directors still working in our theatre – by Byam Shaw, Peter Hall, Peter Brook and Lord Olivier – have a smooth opulence, touched with swagger, that reduces the leading actors to handsome painted faces. They are posed in rich clothes on various levels of complicated sets, and they are backed by a sparkling or a threatening cyclorama. Already this Shakespeare looks dead. Since those days, the doors of the theatre seem to have swung wide open, and a strict decree seems to have banished make-up, destroyed the set poses, and dressed everyone in clothes that could be worn every day. Now photographs are 'action shots', with lines blurred and forms incomplete, just like newspaper photographs of a foreign disaster or candid revelation.

Obviously our theatre has made the plays 'modern' in its own way. There is the Brechtian Shakespeare, with realistic detail and overt dialectic; the Shakespeare with elaborate crowd-scenes based on actors' improvisations; the Shakespeare on swings, trapezes and stilts that give stimulus to actors like the mechanical aids to performance in some of Meyerhold's work in revolutionary Russia. Productions have long-held pauses and unambiguous, pointed stresses, such as a lecturer might use in explaining his point of view to a class of students. There are hints of the bleak, stoical, comical and sensitive isolation that is expressed in Beckett's plays, and of the painful thrust towards exposure that is characteristic of Harold Pinter's characters. We can recognize moments of surprised intimacy and warmth, or climactic outbreaks of aggression, like those which dominate many plays written today in attempts to reveal our present condition of life to our present conditioned attention.

We could not have avoided Shakespeare our contemporary. This is all anyone, any time, has had. Theatre works in this way. A printed book is the same object from one generation to another, so that it changes only in the mind of the individual reader; but a play exists fully only in the human actors, on a stage before an audience – and all these elements are changing all the time. A Shakespeare play seen at the crowded Globe, on a winter's afternoon in the open air, cannot be the same play that is seen by tourists in one or other of the Stratfords, or in some old-fashioned theatre in overcrowded, twentieth-century New York or London. But while modernization is inevitable, obvious and eminently desirable, as the actors, the stages and the audiences all change, there is still some choice in the matter. The recognition of change is an opportunity to judge what we are doing and to ask whether it is to our liking. Is the Shakespeare of our time the only possible one for us? Theatre is resistant to radical change because it is so complicated in operation. It is therefore a very traditional art. If it were to effect an about-face, its organizers, financiers, actors, designers, directors, technicians, audiences and buildings would all have to change, and at the same time. For this reason alone, our Shakespeare may not be modern enough; we may see the plays as they have been inherited from the day before yesterday, changed only in a few surface particulars. The changes which we welcome may have been effected only because they were made where change is easiest to effect.

Of course our critical and scholarly appraisal of Shakespeare is not influenced by these conservative theatrical pressures. This work of presentation has all the freedom and open-mindedness of an individual mind. But here our educational system often brings its own demands and opportunities to the writer, exerting an influence less easy to detect and therefore, perhaps, less easy to resist. Most writers about Shakespeare hold university or school positions, and so their thought and persuasiveness may well be defined, consciously or unconsciously, by professional practice, competition, in-talk and idealism. High among a writer's priorities may be the need to establish his point of view and authority; on the lowest level this can be represented by the catch-phrase 'publish or perish', so that a book on Shakespeare may count directly towards university tenure or advancement; on a higher level, the need to have one's say, to try to sustain an argument at book-length in a way that can speak to other professionals, is like a coming of age, an assumption of responsibility. A further pressure comes from the writer's students, some of whom need to be told what to know in order to pass examinations; it is hard for a teacher to refuse to supply answers.

To write helpfully about Shakespeare is as difficult as to 'make the plays "modern"' in our theatres. Both tasks are not as straightforward as they seem. To a university scholar, the task of a theatre director may seem a matter of honesty, of the need to let Shakespeare speak for himself. Professor Kenneth Muir writing in *Shakespeare Survey* has insisted that the best way to produce Shakespeare in the theatre is to play him 'straight, without cuts and without gimmicks', arguing that Shakespeare always knew better than his adaptors.[1] The words of the text, so this argument goes, are our only reliable clue as to how we should recreate his plays in the theatre, and therefore a director should begin by respecting them. But the text is a most complicated, difficult and inexhaustible clue, a clue that becomes a labyrinth as soon as we approach at all closely. Where should a director begin to respond? What priorities should he allot? Should he start by trying to get the simpler things right, paying first attention to metre, syntax, rhythm, imagery, vocabulary? Or should he begin work by seeking to create an impression of individual character, or of social context? When should he consider the overall argument of the play? How should he respond to ostensible meaning, to subtext or supertext? It is almost impossible to exhaust the implications of ten or twenty lines of Shakespeare's mature writing: if an actor were told to recognize all the clues before he began, he might well never utter a syllable.

A director would recognize the force of a scholar's advice to be faithful to the text, but he would always answer with another question, 'How?' Peter Brook has elaborated on this:

> A director picks up these texts and at once he is responsible. Anything he does becomes a commitment. He cannot avoid this. An actor reads the lines out loud. How? At once a thousand choices are before him. Does he read tonelessly? Does he give the sense with no 'expressive' colour? Does he use the intonations of

[1] 'Shakespeare the Professional', *Shakespeare Survey*, 24 (1971), p. 46.

9

realistic speech? Does he use a special voice? Does he move towards song? ... An actor who speaks must also be seen. How will he appear? How will he be dressed? ... None of these questions can be ducked[1].

In fact both director and scholar share the same dilemma, the need to serve the text, and in their different ways both try to do this. All the innovations of our theatres, including the most eccentric interpretations of single lines by obvious extra-metrical stress or preceding silence, including large cuts, interpolations, funny accents, outrageous clothes or nudity, are all defended and recommended as truth to Shakespeare in our age. Theatre directors, like scholars, pride themselves on truth; but it is truth for the stage, here and now, according to their imagination and technical accomplishments.

To understand how truth can be so conflicting and so constantly varying as the ever-new guises in which Shakespeare's masterpieces appear in production, the role of the director in our theatre must be briefly considered. He is, of course, a new functionary who grew to pre-eminence with the added complication of production methods that followed the introduction of electric light and the elaboration of crowd scenes for emphasis as well as verisimilitude, both influences growing stronger as the nineteenth century drew to its close. From the director comes the organization and unity of concept that is necessary to cope with all the complexity of modern production in fully equipped theatres. But, more than this, he is also responsible for relevance, comprehensibility and 'point of view'. In the nineteen twenties and thirties in Germany, where the value of all aspects of life and art were under searching question, the theatre director stepped forward as a sage. 'The director cannot just be the "servant of the play"', wrote Erwin Piscator in 1926:

> because a play isn't something fixed and final ... the director is allotted the task of finding that standpoint from which he can expose the roots of dramatic creation. ... Only when the director is conscious of his role as the servant and exponent of his age will

1 'Production: Total Responsibility of a Director', *The Birmingham Post*, 17 April 1964.

he be able to fix a standpoint which is in full agreement with the major forces shaping the character of his epoch.[1]

When Lord Olivier wrote to *The Times* to defend a director at the National Theatre from the charge of making 'a wrong-headed reading' of Dogberry in *Much Ado About Nothing*, he made the nub of his argument the 'right' of every director 'to express a point of view on any play': 'in fact', he added, 'that is one of the main things required of him'.[2]

Besides being 'just the servant of the play' and the organizer of its production, the director functions as an interpreter. Like a film camera, his job is to get us to 'see' the play through his eyes. If necessary, he will enlarge, underscore, repeat and eliminate, until no one could fail to see what he is getting at, even if in the process other possibilities are wholly lost to sight. Speaking of a production of *The Tempest* that he would like to direct, Peter Hall gave as his view that

> the real crux of the play is at the end where Miranda says, 'Oh brave new world that has such people in it' and then Prospero says ''Tis new to thee!'

It is relevant to take note that this director was just off to film a version of Aldous Huxley's novel, *Brave New World*, but the importance of his view for any subsequent production that he might undertake must be judged in the light of his further statement:

> Really, audiences like to be jolted – they'll resist it, but deep down inside they like it.[3]

Directors are not only organizers and interpreters, they are also manufacturers and salesmen. They make products that have a clear, easily recognizable image, that arrest attention and seek to satisfy audiences – perhaps indirectly.

To function in this way they need to coin images, to find a new conception for each production of each play. The word

---

1 Quoted in *Erwin Piscator*, Arts Council Exhibition, London, 1971.
2 *The Times*, 18 February, 1965.
3 Interview, *Birmingham Post*, 14 November 1970.

'theme' has become very important, as can be seen in the quotation from *The Empty Space* at the beginning of this chapter. The critic of *The Times* announced that, in Peter Brook's production of *A Midsummer Night's Dream* for the Royal Shakespeare Company in 1970, the 'traditional emphases' had been altered 'to express the main theme' of the play as Brook had discovered it. The critic of *The Observer* reassured her readers with a first sentence:

> Whenever Peter Brook decides to direct a classic, you can be sure that he has some interpretative idea which cuts through the play like a laser.

Plays and Players concluded a long account with a word of hope for the survival of 'our theatre', so 'long as Shakespeare can continue to be as originally reconceived and as happily executed as he is in this *Dream*'.

Listening to directors talk about their work, one might think that Shakespeare's plays were riddles capable of yielding a whole sequence of answers, each one recommended as more surprising, revealing and contemporary than the last. They speak like intellectuals intent on finding some formula to reduce the baffling to the comprehensible, the old to the new, the complicated to the simple. By choosing one fixed viewpoint it is possible to see only one issue in every dramatic conflict, one principle of unity in each detail. In an interview in *Plays and Players*, Jonathan Miller labelled the plays he had directed: so '*King Lear* is about the failure of authority on two levels', he said. For *The Merchant of Venice* which was about to go into rehearsal, the interviewer could report that Mr Miller 'held tightly to a compelling "private theory" about the implications of the play.'[1]

Theatre programmes guide the audience to a conscious recognition of this conceptual unity. The programme for Terry Hands's production of *The Merchant of Venice* at the Royal Shakespeare Theatre in 1971, and a year later at the Aldwych London, announced that the play is about usury, and about 'venturers' in love, commerce and everyday life. John Barton's

[1] *Plays and Players*, March 1970, pp. 52–3.

Othello, produced at the same time at the same theatre, was given a programme with an extended article on the play with a banner headline: 'Hell and Night'. At Stratford, Ontario, in 1972, the 'Director's Notes' for the programme argued that:

> Certain words recur powerfully in *King Lear*: 'nature'; 'nothing'; 'ingratitude'; 'cause'; 'never'; 'patience'; 'love'. They provide a skeleton or silhouette to which the play gives flesh and substance.

David Williams's introduction continued by referring to madness and to contemporary calamities and barbarities. It concluded:

> The play shows us the depths of selfishness and savagery of which human nature is capable. Yet miraculously the last thoughts are not of despair. . . . The consolations within this tremendous play are costly but triumphant.

In such announcements the director seems to share his own search for some governing idea for his production, to reveal the concept with which he has tried to give unity, force, relevance and, sometimes, surprise to his production.

The effect of such an intellectual grasp on the play can be instanced by Peter Brook's *King Lear* at Stratford-upon-Avon in 1962–3. Thanks to the *'Lear* Log' published by his assistant director, Charles Marowitz, this is one of the best documented productions of recent times. Brook laid emphasis on the play's variety of means, but sought a strict unity. Recording their early discussions, Marowitz says that

> for Brook *Lear* is a series of intellectual strands which only performance can tie together. . . . He sees it mainly as a play about sight and blindness.[1]

As the play came alive in rehearsal, Brook shaped and ordered what was discovered; he invented improvisations to help in the elaboration of stage-business, and in the process cut and added to suit his view of the play and ensure a challenging impact on his audience. He decided to prevent any 'reassurance' being

---

[1] 'Lear Log', *Tulane Drama Review*, 8, ii (1963), 103.

given after the blinding of Gloucester, a scene particularly significant for his 'main' theme of 'sight and blindness':

> To remove the tint of sympathy usually found at the end of the Blinding Scene, Brook cut Cornwall's servants and their commiseration of Gloucester's fate. Once the second 'vile jelly' has been thumbed out of his head, Gloucester is covered with a tattered rag and shoved off in the direction of Dover. Servants clearing the stage collide with the confused blind man and rudely shove him aside. As he is groping about pathetically, the house lights come up – the action continuing in full light for several seconds afterwards. If this works, it should jar the audience into a new kind of adjustment to Gloucester and his tragedy. The house lights remove all possibility of aesthetic shelter, and the act of blinding is seen in a colder light than would be possible otherwise.

For the last Act, Brook encouraged the audience to see beyond the text as Shakespeare had written it: Marowitz recorded that:

> At the end of the play, the threat of a reassuring catharsis is even greater. I suggested that, instead of the silence and repose which follows the last couplet, it might be disturbing to suggest that another storm – a greater storm – was on the way. Once the final lines had been spoken, the thunder could clamor greater than ever before, implying that the worst was yet to come. Brook seconded the idea, but instead of an overpowering storm, preferred a faint, dull rumbling which would suggest something more ominous and less explicit.[1]

*   *   *

While a theatre director needs to believe that his conception of a play's theme is the backbone of Shakespeare's creation, it is possible to see it as a confinement, a cutting down of a work founded on something other than an intellectual idea. Certainly this talk of themes has only come into the theatre during the present century, especially within the last few decades. Nor is this surprising for scholars have worked in the same way, re-

[1] Op. cit., p. 114.

interpreting Shakespeare and publishing books on *The Imperial Theme, Justice and Mercy in Shakespeare*, or, more ambitiously still, *The Meaning of Shakespeare*. The comedies, so long enjoyed without conscious moral reflection, have been presented by scholarship as treatments of 'Love's Order', 'Love's Wealth' and 'Love's Truth', each play having its implicit judgement on human relationships.[1] In *Some Shakespearean Themes* (1959), for example, Professor L. C. Knights has given *his* view of *King Lear*:

> if there is one truth that the play brings home with superb force it is that neither man's reason nor his powers of perception function in isolation from the rest of his personality.... *How* Lear feels, in short, is as important as *what* he feels. (p. 100)

Professor Knights acknowledged the limitation of his own viewpoint – 'I shall be mainly concerned with the play's essential significance as I see it' – but nevertheless he spoke with assurance of the 'centre of the action': it is 'the complete endorsement of a particular quality of being'. With certain rather twentieth-century qualifications, he argued that we may call it 'Love' (p. 118). As the director concentrates on one theme that he 'sees', so does the scholar. Perhaps the main difference is that it is easier to see what the director has left out, added, or altered. The similarity between the two is not surprising, for almost all our theatre directors in their younger days have sat – for a short time, and with proper impatience to have their own say – at the feet of university teachers.

Scholars are often concerned to resurrect Elizabethan notions and reactions, but they write for the present generation and are thus quite as much concerned as the director to pluck a comprehensible intellectual heart out of a play. In his *Shakespeare's Tragic Sequence* (1972) Kenneth Muir concluded a chapter on *Macbeth*, which had been concerned with irony, dramatic effect and vocabulary, by pointing to a thematic keystone:

> Amongst other things *Macbeth* is a mirror for magistrates with Duncan, Edward the Confessor and Malcolm serving as *exempla* of the good ruler, and Macbeth himself of the tyrant. (p. 154)

---

[1] See J. R. Brown, *Shakespeare and His Comedies* (1957), *passim*.

15

On *King Lear* he concluded that in this play:

> Shakespeare seems to be considering the possibility that the world is not providentially governed and to be asking 'What then?' The answer he gives is that whether there are gods or not, whether there is an after-life or not in which the wicked are punished and the good rewarded, is almost irrelevant to the question of how we should behave or to the principles on which society should be founded. (p. 141)

Here Shakespeare is seen as an agnostic questioning the answers of other thinkers, and providing his own. It would not be easy to centre a production on this kind of theme, but Muir's formulation could provide a challenge to which a director would know how to respond.

In general, scholars draw out more complex themes. So R. A. Foakes in *Shakespeare: from Satire to Celebration* (1971) saw a sequence of paradoxes in *The Tempest* clarified most fully in the Masque of Ceres and Juno, which thus 'serves as a focus for these paradoxes'. Noting that this masque is a 'stylized and highly structured' entertainment, Foakes saw that it contains:

> the vision of innocence within a pattern involving tradition, myth, history, and social obligation. . . .
>
> It is the vision, like the other wonders and games contrived by art, that gives [the] social and political world its bearings, enables it to understand the relation between nature and civilization, and illustrates the necessity and nature of rule; and finally, it images the moral and religious sanctions necessary for society. (pp. 171–2)

Scholars are also more likely to see ambivalences, and to argue that the plays are exercises in doubt. In *Poison, Play and Duel* (1971), Nigel Alexander described the hero of *Hamlet* as if he were a scholar seeking intellectual assurance. Here the tragedy itself is seen as Shakespeare's examination of a conceptual problem:

> The play closes, as it opened, with the values of Mars. The question that remains is whether the human combination of the values of Mars and Venus is possible or attainable. Mars and Venus meet in the human mind. The play questions whether their union

can ever produce harmony. The argument of the play is over.
The argument about the play has begun. (p. 201)

In *Shakespeare's Early Tragedies* (1968), Nicholas Brooke saw
Hamlet as an exploration of experience and 'ideas' that were
both subtle and sophisticated, 'aided, no doubt, by the reading
of Florio's Montaigne'. For him, the tragedy was both 'complex
and obscure'. The audience must learn to 'see things two ways
round':

> see, surprisingly, that this muddled failure can also be felt as
> triumphant success. (p. 205)

* * *

Neither scholar nor director can be fairly presented by quoting
his most pregnant description of theme or argument; the
descriptions and detailed analysis of the one and the whole
lively and varied production of the other must be taken into
account before such definitions can be judged as keys to
Shakespeare's texts. All that I am seeking to establish here is
the conceptual basis of the work that is done in both theatre
and study. Shakespeare's plays have become plays of ideas:
they are considered in arguments, and they are produced so
that they reflect, at all points, and by every means, a unifying,
relevant and individually perceived theme.

More than this, both scholar and director seek to be relevant
to their age. On taking over the Artistic Directorship of the
Royal Shakespeare Company in 1968, Trevor Nunn acknowledged a common purpose with Dr Leavis, the critic who had
stimulated him as an undergraduate at Cambridge:

> Where I go all the way with Leavis is in his insistence that *all*
> art should directly influence living – the individual's and society's,
> both.
> To me the theatre is a live organism which should be devoted to
> influencing people – not dogmatically, or in any propaganda
> sense – but through a shared experience between actors and
> audience.[1]

[1] Interview, *Sunday Telegraph*, 4 February 1968.

There can be little doubt that both kinds of interpreter, who discern the secret themes of Shakespeare's plays with individual and sometimes challenging clarity, are equally concerned to communicate their visions, to work truthfully and to reach through words or productions the widest possible audience.

But my larger question remains unanswered: do these presenters function in the best way possible for our age and for the inherent qualities of Shakespeare's texts? I shall begin by considering further the ways in which the plays are rehearsed, staged and produced in our theatres, for it is a theatrical life which Shakespeare envisaged for them. Stage reality holds and extends the range of our minds so powerfully that if we are limited there we are almost certainly limited in our own private conceptions of the plays. How do we see Shakespeare in performance?

3

Performance: directors, designers and actors

In establishing his interpretation of a Shakespeare play, the director's strongest ally is the designer. The effects this collaborator creates are large and they make a direct assault on the audience's senses. Usually the two meet for several weeks before rehearsals begin and work out a bold strategy for the production. Stage-settings, costumes, properties and the major light-effects are all planned without the presence of actors so that work can begin in time for completion well before the first night; only small changes or eliminations are possible during the rehearsal period. In this way the designer is in closest and most direct contact with the director's conceptual view of the play, undisturbed by the discoveries of other members of the production company.

During the present century many styles have been used by designers and directors to give visual settings to Shakespeare's plays that outdistance any theatrical effect of which the dramatist could have dreamed. But, increasingly, the use of modern devices has been modified by the designer's knowledge of how the Elizabethan theatre worked: it is a story of adaptation and compromise, the twin pursuits of contemporary viability and period reconstruction. But the compromise has not been easy, for no single line of development is discernible. Rather the quick alterations of style may suggest that the bases of Shakespearian stagecraft have been missed and that our designers are flirting with inessentials.

Taking the Royal Shakespeare Theatre as example, it is clear that in the last dozen or so years the way of setting the plays has changed several times. The year 1959 saw Lila de Nobili's detailed evocation of an Elizabethan mansion for *A Midsummer Night's Dream*. Wooden steps and platform provided equivalents of the inner and upper stages familiar in drawings of the Globe Theatre, but by the means of gauzes and decorations the same basic setting could be transformed to suggest a wood with flowers, leaves and uncertain light. Yet in the same year Tanya Moiseiwitsch set *All's Well That Ends Well* in alternating styles, three-walled interiors changing to smallish three-dimensional scenic units that were wheeled on stage in front of a plain cyclorama. The *Dream* used Elizabethan costumes, predominantly white for the lovers and gold for fairies. *All's Well* used costumes of the early twentieth-century for the courtly scenes, but changed to the Second World War for the military ones. Despite lively farcical humour in many episodes, the last impression of the *Dream* was hazy, processional and glittering: the theatre of marvels and picturesque enchantment. In the final scene of *All's Well*, the director, Tyrone Guthrie, grouped numerous supers within the 'walls' of the setting to accentuate the comic confrontations of the action, notably by a slow, arthritic and morally indignant down-stage cross by the Widow, from the doorway and flunkeys, to the steps, throne and King. The idiom of these productions was mixed: drawing-room comedy, musical comedy, opera perhaps, revue, 'spectaculars'. The common element was showmanship, the presentation of a world that is special to the theatre, using the theatre's recognizable devices, deftly and continuously. Complexions were 'made-up', and costumes remained clean and well-pressed throughout the action, in war or peace, nightmare or reality.

Five years later John Bury was working at Stratford with the director, Peter Hall. This designer had not been trained at Art School, but began working in the nineteen-forties as assistant electrician to Joan Littlewood's touring Theatre Workshop. Moving around from one fit-up to another with the simplest equipment and smallest budget, he found lighting the cheapest way to evoke mood or setting, and the quickest to change a scene. When Littlewood took over the Theatre Royal in Stratford East, London, he created stage sets without the usual paint-and-canvas flats. He preferred real materials, from paving stones and baulks of timber, to junk and ordinary household objects. By 1964, John Bury had moved again to Stratford-upon-Avon and was given the task of setting seven of Shakespeare's history plays for performance in sequence, and with this large undertaking his style became fixed, representing a complete change from the earlier showmanship at this theatre.

Now the stage was bare and level, as spacious and free for movement as the stage at the Globe. But two wall-sections were placed on it that could be moved into almost any position, and so reveal the metal plates, staircases, doorways, trellises or bare boards that were their variable faces. Besides suggesting the location of each scene, these walls could confine the acting-space whenever necessary, for interiors, prison scenes and so forth. But the dramatic action was still further centred on large properties and specially constructed furniture, such as a throne, two huge swords, a prisoner's chain, a council-table, a cask of wine, an altar, or a bed. These objects defined the situation and provided business for the actors, as well as giving a point of visual focus. Repeated appearances of a cart on the field of battle suggested a debt to the Berliner Ensemble's production of *Mother Courage*, but thrones and council-tables were, in fact, still more numerous. This style of setting may owe much to the use of such properties on the Elizabethan stage, as illustrated in the property-lists that have survived.

Further definition of the stage picture was derived from restricted and carefully directed lighting, and its effect was enhanced by using a restrained palette for costumes and scenery, brown, grey and black predominating: so that the actors' faces and occasional patches of lighter colour or white stood out with more than usual clarity. By using real-looking surfaces, especially simulated steel-sheet on the stage floor, the light was variously reflected or absorbed, and so a general indication of atmosphere was achieved that more usually would have been supplied by decoration, gauzes, paint or false perspectives.

For the appearance of the actors, John Bury has said he 'wanted to take the fancy-dress out of costumes'.[1] Period detail was sacrificed to expression of function. Various cloths were treated with metal sprays, gold dust, tennis-court grit and

[1]   See 'Against Falsehood', *Flourish*, 5 (1965), p. 6.

marble chippings, so that the human figures were hard and shiny or, in contrast, crumbling and decayed. Near nakedness for a bedroom alternated with complete armour; a coarse open-weave smock for Henry VI contrasted with a flowing silk robe for Richard II. Little make-up seemed to be used, and that little was more to represent sweat, tiredness, age or infirmity, than to accentuate facial features or generally to glamorize.

This style may be summed up as selective realism, but with as much emphasis on the selection as on the imitation of real human activity. It was plain but stylish, ordinary but impressive, sombre and yet sharply pointed. At times the setting operated in defiance of the words, especially for scenes of pastoral lightness or ceremonial splendour: the armies, for instance, were never 'all plumed like estridges' or 'gorgeous as the sun at midsummer' (*I. H4*, IV. i. 98–102). Moreover the emphasis on stage-business for scene-setting slowed down productions. The bringing on of new pieces of furniture, the moving of walls and the enactment of physical tasks all took time, and on the wide, deep and uncluttered stage, there were long distances to be covered. Some of the shorter scenes seemed to take as long to set as to play. Individual plays took 15 to 45 minutes longer to perform than in earlier seasons.[1] For *Hamlet* of the following year, also designed by John Bury and directed by Peter Hall, the detailed realism was taken still further, slowing up the pace and, in domestic situations, introducing a fussy emphasis on silent actions that had been less obvious in the action-crammed Histories: Polonius stops to look up references in books, Laertes neglects Ophelia to pack his bags for Paris, Polonius sips and savours his wine, Polonius supplies Claudius with appropriate papers.

Some productions at Stratford in these years were designed by Koltai and Sally Jacobs, who both used stronger colours and bolder effects: dark green was dominant in *Love's Labour's Lost*, yellow, white and sharp blue in the first half of *Timon*, blood-

[1] According to the programmes and discounting intervals, *First Part of Henry IV* played 160 minutes in 1951, 180 minutes in 1964; the *Second Part* played 165 minutes in 1951, 180 in 1964; *Hamlet* played 175 minutes in 1956, 220 minutes in 1965.

red, orange and stone for the Venetian scenes of *The Merchant of Venice* with sky-blue and white for the Belmont scenes. Here the effect was too single-minded for the variety implicit in Shakespeare's texts: *Love's Labour's Lost* could not move from lightness and warmth to a chill evening because the tall, dark forms of the yew hedges that flanked the stage had, from the outset, suggested that 'the scene' had already begun 'to cloud' (V. ii. 710). Stark purity of colour in the Belmont scenes of *The Merchant* viewed against the blue cyclorama made for coldness and clarity, so that wit became forced and the intermittent expressions of gentler sentiment quite lost.

When Trevor Nunn took over the directorship of the Royal Shakespeare Theatre he soon evolved a new style with his new chief designer, Christopher Morley. The stage was stripped and its absolute limits marked by a huge three-sided box without a top. The director and designer could not imitate Shakespeare's platform stage set within a wooden 'O', so they set about creating what they called a 'chamber' for their own kind of theatre. In this way they hoped to establish:

> that the most important object on the stage is the actor: . . . what he wears, what he sits on, possessions directly connected with him, are the next important point. The middle and far distances are not important. We've abandoned flying scenery. We want the stage to represent earth, (as for the Elizabethans) and underneath that stage lies hell, the unknown, the darkly occult. Above it is a canopy, a roof fretted with golden fire, the gods, heaven, Apollo. Creating a very simple universe has meant reorganizing the lighting – the stage is now lit like a billiard table from above.[1]

Although Trevor Nunn used the verbal language of Shakespeare's day to describe his intentions, the basic stage that Christopher Morley devised looked up-to-the-minute: modish, bright, clean and artificial. When its floor was fitted with carpet or with white rectangles of synthetic smoothness, and when the whole was brightly lit from above and a few actors dressed all in one or two colours were posed within it, the stage looked like a vast shop-window from Harrods, Sacks of Fifth

[1] Trevor Nunn, in interview, *Plays and Players*, September 1970, p. 17.

Avenue, or some other expensive shopping store, or like a double-page spread in the advertising section of a glossy consumer's magazine or Sunday Supplement.

Some of these associations were probably welcomed, or even pursued, by the company, for implicit in the notions behind this form of staging is the need to display, and to find a 'contemporary' image. But since this 'chamber' staging was first used in 1969 changes in its employment obviously show the main shortcomings that the theatre company itself has discovered. Chief of these is that such a set dwarfs the actors that the designer intended to display: its height goes right up into the flies, its width and depth maximize the spaciousness of the stage; and, for many scenes, no large stage property or independent piece of scenery had been allowed to break the extended, straight lines. Audibility problems were increased, and it was hard for a comic to reach out to his audience unless he played consistently to the front, losing contact with his fellow actors. Moreover any inadequacy in the physical realization of a role was accentuated by the bare, sharp and bright setting. For some actors, this may have been a useful challenge, as Pericles took a full minute to walk around the stage towards a fateful meeting, or as Hermione was seen in profile crossing the back of the 'chamber' before making a right-angled turn to walk slowly and silently down stage to confront her husband and judge in the Trial Scene. Bearing, tempo, music or silence can impress the effect of such an entry or confrontation, inescapably – although often at the cost of the balance and rhythm of the scene as a whole as Shakespeare's text sustains it. But if the actor's physical performance is less than perfect, the effect is disturbed by any eccentric detail; if he uses a routine, empty posture, this use of the chamber-stage accentuates a portentous directorial purpose. Scenes involving only second-line actors, as the return from the oracle in *The Winter's Tale* (III. i.) or the first moments of *Hamlet*, are particularly vulnerable to this kind of exposure, especially if the production is as static as in the Oracle Scene at Stratford. While this style of staging accentuates the actor, it can also dwarf him and accentuate his failings when he appears alone or nearly alone.

The Royal Shakespeare Theatre's response to these difficulties was seen in the last two productions of the 1969 season for which a smaller acting area was marked off within the huge chamber, for *Twelfth Night* by a diminishing tunnel of lattice work, vaguely suggesting a garden and opening towards the audience, and for *Henry VIII* by confining the action to an octagon fully down stage, while placing right across the back of the chamber a small-scale silhouette of Tudor London against which human figures seemed more than usually tall. In 1970 and 1971 almost all the plays were given some background of trellis, screens, or movable, three-dimensional units that limited the acting space within the bright, wide, revealing shop-window. In 1972, the stage-floor was made flexible, so that walls, steps, ramps and podiums could limit the acting-space in various ways and thrust the actors towards the audience.

Throughout these seasons selected realism gave way to overt statement about the play's 'themes', the ideas that the director had observed in the play and chosen to bring into prominence. So the stage properties, 'possessions' and clothes, with which Trevor Nunn intended to take the eye, did not serve the realistic purposes familiar in John Bury's stage sets. Now they also provided 'keys' or dominant 'images' for each scene. In *The Winter's Tale* the instability of Leontes' character was demonstrated by setting the first scene among outsized nursery toys, a rocking-horse and building bricks, all in purest white. In Act II, scene iii, Leontes sat with a huge white chess-board set for an unfinished game, and lying on stage was a white doll with a blackened eye. The costume that Polixenes wore in the first scene changed colour from brown to lurid red as a special lighting effect was introduced: this was used to show the audience, unmistakably, the nightmare reality that Leontes imagines when he thinks he sees his friend's sexual play with Hermione, his Queen.

In all but one production lights were openly used for directorial comment, as Christopher Morley explained in interview:

> we have a great 20 kilowatt light above the stage rains down light in a soft, irridescent way and another similar one over the fore-stage – Apollo One and Two we call them. You can also carve

into this at any point with a spotlight – it sounds old-fashioned but in fact the follow-spot is really the most Shakespearean of devices in that it helps one achieve the same kind of focus as the actor can achieve by underscoring a single line.[1]

To give a nightmare quality to the battles at the end of *Richard III*, the stage was darkened and individual figures picked out, intermittently, with moving and momentary spotlights. In *Hamlet*, the first court scene was established as a public-relations job by having the main characters stand in row along the front of the stage in a box of intense light, like that used for television appearances. In all these cases, the set and lighting achieved what would normally – and, in Elizabethan times, necessarily – have come from the performances. While supposed to support the actor, the designer has here taken over from him.

Costumes sometimes imitated twentieth-century fashions, wholly in *Winter's Tale* or for *The Merchant of Venice* of 1971, or for the occasional coat or shirt in *Hamlet*, or for the underwear of the comics in *The Tempest*. Like John Bury, these designers avoid fancy-dress wherever possible, but not to make the set look lived-in, rather to present the action in immediately recognizable terms. The palette of colours is also restricted, but not to give a variable texture to the picture, rather to make oppositions between characters more evident than their words and actions could alone achieve. So Hamlet was all in black, until he leaves Elsinore for England, as in most productions; but here the designer also put everyone else all in white. On his return Hamlet was in white, and everyone else in black. The designer had drawn the same line between Hamlet and Ophelia, or Hamlet and Gertrude, as between Hamlet and Claudius, or Rosencrantz, or Osric: so he isolated Hamlet more than Shakespeare's text implies, and in unmistakable manner. In *The Tempest* the court party were in uniform rust and gold, while Miranda and Prospero were in clothes bleached to uniform neutrality. The spirits of the island were almost naked and whitish, no colour being introduced for Iris, Ceres or Juno, no

[1] 'The Designer Talks', interview with Michael Billington, *Plays and Players*, January 1970, p. 54.

warmth for the 'sun-burnt sicklemen of August weary' (IV. i. 134). The designer and director were intent on emphasizing the spirit-human dichotomy of the play, and the suffering of Prospero. So the 'many-coloured' enchantment of an imaginary world was submerged in a simple colour scheme that served one idea.

Sally Jacobs's set for Peter Brook's production of *A Midsummer Night's Dream* (1970) took the company style still further. Her innovations were to make the acting space smaller, insetting a three-sided white box so that around it and above it there was an area in which music could be played, stage tricks set in motion, and actors be seen to prepare, or to watch and react to their fellows in the play itself. The stage properties and representations of bushes and trees were still less realistic: trapezes, swings, wooden stilts, coiled wires, two plain oblong white doorways of equal size and spacing, black metal ladders down the front at either side of the stage, a black handrail round the top. This was a machine for acting in. A white light remained almost unchanged throughout the play, whether in Athens or wood, by night or day. Actors were again exposed in sharpest outline, and this effect was accentuated by costumes of simple cut, many of them in white and one or two sharp colours. The lack of realistic or atmospheric illusion, together with the obvious inventiveness of the stage-business and the new antics of the performers, were a constant challenge to the audience. Never could they imagine that they had strayed into a slice of life, nor even into an enlarged, simplified and more essential version of aspects of real life. The ingenious, theatrical construction had to be taken – or rejected – as a transformation of life. Not surprisingly Meyerhold was quoted in the printed programme:

> There is a fourth *creator* in addition to the author, the director and the actor – namely, the spectator ... from the friction between the actor's creativity and the spectator's imagination, a clear flame is kindled.

By creating a kind of clean, stark gymnasium or circus for the setting of this production, the director and designer ignored many of the words of the text, especially the ambiguous, gentle and homely words in which the play abounds.

*   *   *

This brief history of stage-design for Shakespeare during a dozen or so years could be paralleled, with local variations, in accounts of other theatres. Most of today's theatre designers have been trained in schools that are geared to quick changes of visual fashions, in clothes, furnishings and art. They live in a world of display and competition, and are familiar with hoardings, television-commercials and coloured advertisements. All these influences are reflected in their designs for the stage, wrought at the same pitch, with the same assertiveness and eye-catching novelty. Even if they wished to resist these pressures, it would be hard to do so for they use the same technical resources: strong and flexible light, paint sprays, large sheets of plastic material, nylon, terylene and other synthetic cloths. The mounting cost of labour necessitates the use of mechanical preparation and large untreated surfaces, and the absence of hand-made detail. Habitually, technically and financially, stage designers are committed to the effect of 'blow-up'. As sets become more fashionable, simpler and less expensive to make, so they become exaggerated and exaggerating. A throne alone on a shiny black stage is unavoidable, portentous. An actor alone is exposed, and must simplify his performance greatly if he does not wish to look insignificant, fussy or in-efficient. A change of lighting can make the actor disappear from view. In all this, the effect is not so much theatrical or stagey as overtly *effective*: any actor can be impressive, and any small hand-property dominate the stage.

As a response to the detailed demands of Shakespeare's texts with their ambiguities, suggestiveness, and very human variety, such a style is affected, simple-minded and unambiguous. It limits meaning and suppresses histrionic excitement. It is a fake world of dummies, or a mindless world of sensuous excitement. For all its lip-service to Elizabethan precedent, its chief merit is that it reflects an aspect of the contemporary world displayed outside the theatre in homes, shops and journals.

If this criticism seems to cut right across current stage practice, especially as shown at Stratford-upon-Avon, strong support can be found from the pronouncements of the very directors who work at that theatre. The programme for *The Tempest* (1970) bore this quotation from Coleridge (1812):

> In this play Shakespeare has especially appealed to the imagination, and he has constructed a plot well adapted to the purpose. According to his scheme, he did not appeal to any sensuous impression . . . of time and place, but to the imagination, and it is to be borne in mind that of old, and as regards mere scenery, his works may be said to have been recited rather than acted – that is to say, description and narration supplied the place of visual exhibition: the audience was told to fancy that they saw what they only heard described; the painting was not in colours, but in words.

The same critic is quoted to much the same effect in the programme for Peter Brook's *Dream*, but with further comment by the American scholar, C. L. Barber:

> The nearly bare stage worked as Proust observed that the bare walls of an art gallery worked, to isolate 'the essential thing, the act of mind'.

Peter Hall, in discussing plans for the Royal Shakespeare Company's new London theatre in the Barbican, opposed actors to spectacle:

> Theatre is certainly actors, but not necessarily scenery. This is the most important consideration today. An actor, with good evocative words, can stimulate an audience to imagine Ancient Rome far more readily than a complete and beautifully built set. But the actor's background must not *contradict* our imaginations. Bare boards and black curtains can kill our imaginings. They are arid. But a pillar that is a meaningful symbol of the whole town, or a suggestive texture, can help the actor. But they should not take over his job.[1]

Peter Hall recommends compromise and tact, but such a pillar as he describes can dwarf an actor and limit the audience's

[1] 'Towards the Barbican', *Flourish*, 6 (1966), p. 2.

concept of a city at least as much as any more complicated set, and arguably more. It can also create a showy ambience for the actor in which simplification and enlargement of his performance are not only appropriate, but positively necessary. Any effective setting is bound to work against the theory of the directors that the actors should dominate: such settings speak forcibly and continuously for themselves.

Perhaps some of the difficulties arise from Coleridge's notion that 'words' are the opposite of 'spectacle'. Peter Hall's contrast between 'actors' and 'scenery' is more helpful, but he goes on quickly to suppose that 'good evocative words' are the actor's means of communication. If the actor's total performance, in contact with other actors and dominating the audience's attention, is opposed to the theatre of stage-display, then the predicament of the designer becomes more evident. Shakespeare's plays live in and with the actors, and in the audience's reaction to their performances. Always Shakespeare imagined characters and actions 'on a stage', or on a 'scaffold'. There was *no* 'meaningful' background: there was *no* 'style' for a production; there was not even a designer.

In our day, when the Elizabethan theatre is dead beyond recall, the first task for a designer is to discover a way of setting Shakespeare which allows the actor to dominate. He must be the most noticeable element in the production, the most suggestive, challenging and exciting. He must be fully alive and free. The problem is not to find a suggestive prompting for the audience's imaginative creation of a 'background': the plays themselves have no background. If it is argued that we now need a background for any figure, because our visual senses have developed away from Elizabethan habits of sight, then the background must lack precise meaning, and must not directly relate to what is happening between actor and actor. After all, we are still capable of viewing human beings, and we are perhaps newly perceptive in this task that is sufficiently exciting and unpredictable to hold attention for three hours of performance.

That human activity was the centre of focus in Shakespeare's theatre, as well as words, is attested by various accounts of acting at that time. Indeed it might be true to say that performances were as much 'dances' as 'recitations'. An anonymous writer in 1616 contrasted an orator and actor:

> as an Orator was most forcible in his elocution; so was an actor in his gesture and personated action.[1]

When Buckingham in *Richard III* sneeringly speaks of a tragedian, he gives a list of gestures:

> Tut, I can counterfeit the deep tragedian,
> Speak and look back, and pry on every side,
> Tremble and start at wagging of a straw:
> Intending deep suspicion, ghastly looks
> Are at my service, like enforced smiles. (III. v. 5–9)

In *The Two Gentlemen*, Julia speaks of performing Ariadne's 'passioning . . . which I so lively acted with my tears', that her audience 'wept bitterly' (IV. iv. 163–7): there is nothing here of what she *said*. In a note to the published version of *The White Devil* (1612), John Webster seems to use the word 'action' for 'performance', saying that for an 'imitation of life' it was 'the best that ever became them'. It was reported that a company of English actors touring in Germany were followed from one town to another by an audience that 'understood not their words' and came 'only to see their action'.[2]

Few of the stage directions in the first edition of the plays are certainly Shakespeare's own and most of these do little to define the nature of performance. But *Coriolanus* and *Antony and Cleopatra* were first printed from manuscripts which were probably prepared by the author himself to give some impression of the action.[3] In the former, a domestic scene in the hero's home is prefaced by the direction: 'They sit them down on two low stools and sew' (I. iii. 1), the word 'low' being an efficient indication of posture. At the entry to the Senate in II. ii., a list of characters is followed by '*Scicinius and Brutus take their places by themselves: Coriolanus stands.*' Here two isolated and one standing figure give physical contrast within a large formal group. When Menenius goes to persuade Coriolanus to spare

---

[1] T.G., *The Rich Cabinet* (1616), Q4.
[2] F. Moryson, *Shakespeare's Europe*, ed. C. Hughes (1903), p. 304.
[3] See W. W. Greg, *The Shakespeare First Folio* (1955), pp. 398–407.

the city of Rome, Shakespeare uses a form of entry direction that is common in plays of the period: '*Enter Menenius to the Watch or Guard*' (V. i. i.). The old politician does not enter an enemy camp, but confronts the soldiers; and in that meeting is sufficient identification of place and situation. In *Antony and Cleopatra*, two directions fourteen lines apart show Shakespeare concerned with contrasts of action: '*Enter the Guard rustling in, and Dolabella*', and then '*Enter Caesar with all his train, marching*' (V. ii. 323 and 337).

In modern productions much of the scene-setting is achieved by large casts of supers engaged in illustrative actions, filling out the stage-picture created by the designer. The effect of this is illustrated in the usual productions of *Henry V*. The play lives in our theatres as a dramatic exploration of battle, with sword-fights, gunsmoke and a visual and aural evocation of war in either Elizabethan or twentieth-century terms. A large cast is carefully drilled to avoid danger and act with maximum effect, and the sound-effects, property and scenic departments work overtime. Often we are shown a few clips of battlefield newsreels to the accompaniment of very loud stereophonic recordings of music, screams and explosions. With something of a quiet shock we turn back to the play-text and realize that *Henry V* is one of the few history plays without armed conflict. There are speeches urging men to fight, debates and truces, official defiances and long accounting for the dead, but no actual fighting. Shakespeare was pursuing a quieter game than our designers and directors, the conflict within men and the relationship of man to man. In fact, as a battle-play *Henry V* is poorly organized, a long time beginning and a long time ending. But as a play about its hero's public face and private self, his influence, responsibility, ignorance, isolation and crises of thought and feeling, excitement is sustained to the end. It starts with an enigmatic king, skilful in political argument and yet vibrant with anger: condemning traitors, he weeps; before battle he seeks talk, soliloquy and then urgent prayer. When he is ready for the fight, he makes a virtue of danger and asserts kinship with every man in his army. He wrangles, mocks and kisses his way to marriage with the daughter of his enemy. Other characters on-stage provide contrasts, and display their own inner contradictions and resolutions. It is a play teeming with sharp, demanding, surprising, individualized, dramatic life, not a panorama of battle-scenes.

In a large modern theatre, designed for the audience to be seated in parallel rows facing a picture-frame opening and, behind that, a composed picture, the designer has had to devise comprehensive settings for Shakespeare's plays. He cannot dispense with scenery so that the play is performed against a neutral background. Light or dark, tall, short or broad, the whole picture would still count: grouping, long entries, large dimensions could not be avoided, and would continue to make their large effects. Any property introduced into this picture would gain disproportionate attention. In most twentieth-century theatres the plays are inevitably seen as in a show-case which magnifies all objects indiscriminately, so that the human beings on whom the drama depends simplify for effect, and enlarge a single, unambiguous response: anything else would look fussy, trivial, mistaken.

A large open-stage, with an audience all one side, presents much the same problems. A thrust stage or an arena decreases the importance of background, but in large modern theatres of this kind, with the stage brightly lit and the audience of some two thousand or so, sitting in rows in the dark, a picture is contrived by means of costume and properties that can be seen clearly from the most distant seat. Usually a production on this type of stage outdoes in splendour, elaboration and variety that of a picture-frame stage, as if striving to compensate for the lack of background and for that security of effect which can be contrived when the audience faces all one way.

However much the individual display styles of the designers may seem at variance with the complexity of Shakespeare's writing and the emphasis which Shakespeare and Elizabethan theatre-practice placed upon the actors, they are, certainly, the most convenient, apt and unmistakable means by which the director can enforce his concept of each individual play. The choice of the right designer is as important to him as the casting of the principal roles. Besides making its own statement, the setting provides the key for the whole composition, stretches the actors in some ways and limits them in others.

Lila de Nobili's set for *A Midsummer Night's Dream* emphasized the artificiality of an ordered world and the childishness that was revealed through dream and fantasy. John Bury's set for the Histories allowed the director to emphasize power and cruelty, reducing human aspiration, idealism and affection in favour of those qualities which are appropriate to a very intelligent horror-comic. If a director decides that *Hamlet* is about 'appearance and reality', then the set will be full of reflecting surfaces and silently moving forms, as for the Prospect Theatre's production of 1971. If *The Merchant of Venice* is about money, love and death, then the set will be successively casket, play-pit and tomb, as at Stratford-upon-Avon in 1971 where the background alternately shone with gold and shimmered with heavenly blue. If a director wishes to show how alike various characters are, the designer will provide costumes that are almost indistinguishable from each other, so that a Duke looks like a lackey, a boy like a girl, a monster like a man. At Stratford, Connecticut, in 1972, all the senators and citizens in *Julius Caesar* wore uniforms of straight, narrow and white tunics or togas, the one major contrast being provided by the military costumes: these were huge beetle-like structures in leather and plastics. To accentuate the hieratic and impersonal nature of the first court-scene in *King Lear*, designers at the Stratfords of England and Canada in 1969 and 1972 provided complicated and glittering garments with long trains borne by many attendants. Not only do such costumes make obvious and unambiguous statements on the director's behalf, but they restrict the movements and physical expressiveness of the actors to a minimum; everything is subservient to the statement of an overall, unifying purpose.

The designer also works with the director in creating the acting-style of a production. The gymnasium with its trapezes which Sally Jacobs provided for Brook's *Dream*, forced the actors into unfamiliar physical activity, calling forth energy, invention and unexpected discoveries. For *The Merchant of Venice* at the National Theatre, London, in 1970, Julia Trevelyan Oman provided a Victorian setting which gave to the Belmont scenes the mannerisms of a befrilled and overdecorated parlour. So Portia fluttered her eyes, smiled and waited for footmen and chambermaids to precede her; she spoke softly and even seemed to blush. By-play was elaborate, and so Arragon pulled a knotted handkerchief out of his pocket, saw the knot and could not remember what he should remember; he dropped a lump of sugar, a footman picked it up and swallowed it, and the audience laughed again. The critic of *The Times* took the point: the director, Jonathan Miller, had chosen this setting because it emphasized 'the obvious financial element of the play; and it also unmasks the romantic element as so much flimsy sentimental decoration'.

With the designer's aid special business can be introduced to make a point that is not explicit in the text. So for the first witches' scene in *Macbeth* at the Royal Shakespeare Theatre in 1967, John Bury provided a large crucifix which the witches held upside-down while it flowed with blood. The stage was covered with shaggy red rugs, so that the whole stage could seem steeped in tactile bloodiness. From underneath these rugs, as the lights came more forcefully into play, the soldiers of the next scene emerged, almost as uncannily as the witches had hovered in the darksome 'air'. The director had seen the play as an exercise in primitive religion and horror, and his designer was using the suggestive and compelling means of the theatre to enforce this reading.

On a smaller scale the designer also collaborates with the director in the pointing of particular lines in the text, so that a desired interpretation is made conclusively. In the National Theatre *Merchant of Venice*, Laurence Olivier appeared as Shylock in frock-coat and top hat, but when he calls Tubal to meet him at 'our synagogue' to persecute his revenge (III.i. 111), he changed into another creature by ceremoniously donning a Jewish woven robe that transformed his outward appearance. No one in the audience could doubt the religious and racial motivation of his subsequent exit, although in the text his words are also full of murder, money and merchandise. In Act II of *Richard III*, Edward IV leaves the stage after hearing of the death of Clarence with the unremarkable words: 'Come, Hastings, help me to my closet. Ah, poor Clarence!' (II. i. 133). The line might imply pity, weariness, self-awareness, fear, or possibly a new resolution, but Terry Hands, the director at Stratford, wished to show one unambiguous effect, that life existed over against death. His designer, Farrah, provided a wooden tub for the king, who has been kneeling before a crucifix, to push over: it rolled so that it opened towards the audience and out of it tumbled a heap of human skulls. Concern for the tormented king was lost as the audience grasped the general implication – the intellectual point – of this *coup de théâtre*.

A change of lighting is quite sufficient to make such a point, at the director's decision. So in the Royal Shakespeare production of *Othello* when it was seen at the Aldwych Theatre, London, in 1972, several scene-changes were effected in the second half of the play while Iago remained on stage, the only illuminated figure on the darkened stage. At moments when Shakespeare has given him no words to speak, and at that part of the play when he has no further long soliloquies with which to make a direct impression on the audience, the director and designer made sure that Iago's posture and face were noted by the audience so that these could speak for him.

*   *   *

With or without his designer's aid, the director in our theatre is intent all the time upon making his conception of the play clear, unambiguous and strong. To do this he must control his actors, working for both group and individual effects, and choosing from the often baffling ambiguity and variety of Shakespeare's text that aspect of its meaning or implication that suits his chosen purpose. So the actors know which way to work and they are able to build up a performance of striking power. So, too, the audience will know where to look and when to pay most attention.

How much can be achieved in this way may be illustrated by Buzz Goodbody's production of *King John* for the Royal Shakespeare Company in 1970. She directed that the characters should enter marching like toy soldiers, that they should smirk, giggle and repeat phrases in parrot-like chorus. They prayed in unison with mechanical gestures and toneless voices. Blanche's wedding was proposed with humorous over-emphasis and, at the end, a comic 'phew' was introduced to the text. For his death-scene, the king was carried on stage lumped unceremoniously over a lord's back. The director wished to stress the repetitions, self-satisfaction and self-interest of politics, and she did so with wearying completeness. The suffering, uncertainty, passion and moral considerations, so often suggested by the text, were crowded out, submerged in what the director was telling us.

In his production of *Hamlet* at the same theatre in the same year, Trevor Nunn directed Ophelia to try to kiss Hamlet in the nunnery scene: there was a long pause before Hamlet exclaimed with strength: 'It hath made me mad' (III. i. 147). The director told an interviewer that he was examining in this production the 'shifts between real madness and performed madness unknown to the person in the middle of it all'.[1] The 'enterprise of great pitch and moment', the relationships with others, the suspicion, guilt, philosophical concern with the nature of human existence, all of which can be seen in the text, were not his concern: they were not allowed to challenge the clear 'line' through the play's action that director had chosen. In this production, after the closet-scene with his mother, Hamlet appeared almost naked, and the king gave him two forceful blows in the crutch: the reasons for this change of dress and sudden brutality are harder to discern. Perhaps Hamlet found himself making an obscene gesture or exposure; perhaps he was trying to find a new activity by shedding his mourning, and Claudius was simply taking the nearest way to stopping him for the moment. But clearly the director had turned Shakespeare's ironic, challenging and uneasy scene into some sort of physical, man-to-man opposition. (Perhaps the director had read R. D. Laing on *Aggression*, while investigating madness for his production.) The director was interpreting the scene in the light of his own 'fascination' with the possibilities of the text and had found a physical way of making an unprecedented statement; whatever that statement was meant to say, it overwhelmed anything that was actually said or merely implied.

Some directors are particularly fond of enforcing their view

[1] Interview, *Plays and Players*, September 1970, pp. 16–17.

of a play by breaking speeches with silences, or by heavy emphasis on a few words, or by some eye-arresting gesture accompanying them. John Barton of the Royal Shakespeare Company works in this way, so that actors in his productions become unusually effective in their use of words. Sometimes he underlines what is already plain enough, as in Angelo's reply to Isabella's departing, 'Save your honour!' in *Measure for Measure* (II. ii. 161): here the text reads, 'From thee; even from thy virtue!', which could be said within the same iambic verse-line as Isabella's last words. Ian Richardson, however, in the 1970 production spoke it with a long pause after 'thee' which gave the last phrase overwhelming emphasis. At the end of *The Tempest*, John Barton found that he wanted to emphasize Prospero's farewell to Ariel more than Shakespeare had done. The conclusion of the text has Prospero asking the courtiers to 'draw near', implying a general *exeunt*, but in Barton's production the words were transposed, and after a pause, as Antonio and Sebastian *leave* Prospero, rather than join him, the farewell to the spirit was gravely and slowly said as the new conclusion to the play.

A delayed exit is one of the most common devices for emphasizing one aspect of the text. In John Barton's production of *Measure for Measure*, Isabella did not go out with duke or brother at the close of the play, but remained for a silent soliloquy, which marked her undeniably as the odd one out. At the end of *The Merchant of Venice* at the National Theatre both Jessica and Antonio were left on stage after the group *exeunt*, each reading the letter Portia has just given them: Jessica took longer than the Merchant to leave, and as she went, sadly, a voice was heard singing off-stage a Jewish song suitable both for death and bridal. Jonathan Miller, the director, had insisted that the audience went away counting the cost of happiness, despite the fact that the text of the play ends with a bawdy joke from Gratiano. Robin Phillips's production of *The Two Gentlemen* at Stratford-upon-Avon ended with a silent tableau as all the characters remained on stage where Shakespeare's text asks for an *exeunt*; at this point the director introduced a further character, a silent, black-visaged Launce who slowly threaded his way through the silent figures.

Silent business and gestures can be immediately effective, and they are often given prominence over words. In *Richard III*, the director, Terry Hands, cut the Scrivener scene (III. vi.) and kept Richard on stage, silent: he felt pain in his deformed leg and in a long silence he struggled for control; he became fretful and childish. The director had decided to make the audience consider the grounds of motivation at this point: Shakespeare's scrivener, who shows both a man and common humanity, morality and cynicism, perhaps pathos, and certainly irony, was sacrificed in order to build up a particular view of the central character.

In the Prospect Company's production of *Hamlet* attention was drawn as much by the director's invention of stage business as by the performances, or by how the character seems to live in Shakespeare's words and action. The critic of *The Times* noted that Gertrude

> is shown as a flower-lover, always bestowing little bunches on exit: she likes things to be pretty. So for her, the closet scene becomes a real turning point, after which she repulses Claudius with nausea and takes to drink to blot out the situation. With the return of Laertes she has gone to pieces; and is pushed right over the brink by Ophelia's madness. The two of them sit giggling on the floor, playing with flowers. . . . Nothing else in the production approaches this piece of insight.

The same company's *Much Ado About Nothing* in Edinburgh 1970 concluded with Don John brought back on stage, to be shot with a pistol by Don Pedro before he spoke the last words, 'Strike up the pipers'.

Such directorial inventions together with a clear, unifying line throughout a play ensure that each time we go to the theatre we see a new *Much Ado*, a new *Richard III*, a new *Merchant of Venice*, or whatever. When the production is good, each effect will be convincing in its context, capable at that moment of seeming both inevitable and surprising, and in the three hours or more of performance adding to the developing interest of the production. Shakespeare under these conditions is a chameleon dramatist whose works take on ever new colours and new meanings. When the devices are examined out of context and in comparison with the text or with those of other productions, they may lose their eloquence and magic, like a stone that gleamed at the bottom of a stream but turned dull and unremarkable in the hand that gathered it. Moreover the difficulties of a text, due to the passage of time or the complexity of Shakespeare's imagination, are kept out of view, so that the audience follows easily; they are conducted through the play as through an ancient monument, so that they pay most attention to those elements to which their guides believe that they can most easily respond.

When a production is less sure of itself, the edifice can suddenly crumble; it may seem to be always striving for effect and, at the same time, indulging whatever it has discovered that worked for the moment. So after seeing the Royal Shakespeare Company's production of *Henry VIII* at the Aldwych in December 1970, a member of the audience might well be left asking questions. Must Wolsey actually fall to the ground heavily and stiffly when he 'falls' in a political sense? Must the nobles seem so uniform, the political issues so sketchy, men's passions so limited? Should Buckingham alone sustain utterance with rhetorical energy? Should the King play only for simple humour or self-interest, without suggesting underlying purpose and self-awareness? Should Cranmer's lack of polish seem coltish to the degree of stupidity and boorishness? Is it right for the play to finish, not with Shakespeare's last scene, but with King, new Queen and Archbishop, together with a few courtiers, facing the audience to repeat variously, 'peace, plenty, love, truth', and then singing these words rapturously? Why continue this chorus as the King stands alone holding the baby? Must this one obvious point be made still more obvious? Are Shakespeare's plays best performed when actors and audience submit to a simple overall conception and point of view arrived at by the director after private study of the text?

*   *   *

Without a director's guidance to lead a production all one way, most actors would feel lost, unsure which of the myriad of possibilities discovered in their private study, rehearsals, improvisations and day-dreams they should hold on to. They have learnt that power and reassurance come from working in a team towards a clearly defined end. They know that they will be able to hold a silence or take some lines very quietly without interference from other actors on stage, or that a great cross, or a sword, or a capsule of stage blood, lies ready for them to enforce a particular meaning with a surprising visual statement. More than this, they know the main line of their characterization will be sustained throughout the production and contrasted and supported by other members of the company. They know what to expect from lighting, music, sound effects, crowd movements, properties, costumes and so forth; they are free to grow in confidence and expressiveness within the mould, or around the backbone, that has been provided.

The danger, of course, is that the actors may rely too much on what is provided for them and so cease to explore their roles with that creativity or energy which allows them to live on the boundaries of the possible, which surprises their audiences – and themselves – with new and thrilling performances. In these conditions an alert artistic conscience is necessary to keep a carefully prepared and controlled performance fresh and developing.

The director, Peter Brook, has made notable experiments in rehearsal methods to encourage creative imagination in his actors. He does not enunciate a clear conceptual purpose when he starts work. He refuses to 'take a categorical position' in approaching a production:

> I often drive people mad by not making up my mind, but I don't believe it's really a fault. In a work context, the eventual clarity I hope for comes not from any dogmatism, but an encouraged chaos from which the clarity grows.[1]

The first step towards one of his productions is a series of exercises for the actors, physical, vocal, and improvisational, which aim at making the 'actors work more freely together as a group'. The next is to seek a 'collective understanding' of the

[1] 'Showman Extraordinary', an interview with John Heilpern, *The Observer*, 10 August 1970.

play, by using specific acting methods to explore the text through voice and body, through experiment in action. Instead of thinking about the meaning of words, the actors are encouraged to see how they can speak them, represent, support or contrast them. They criticize each other's work and wait for something to come right. Peter Brook tells the story of experimental rehearsals for *The Tempest*, when:

> a Japanese actor who, by approaching Ariel through his breathing and through his body, made Ariel something very understandable. A certain force became tangible in something which to the Japanese was easy to understand because in the basis of the Noh theatre, from which he came, there was a certain type of cry, a certain type of breath. The idea of that force was truly represented. It could be discussed because it had suddenly happened. There it was amongst us. It was no longer force, an abstract movement, it was *force*, a reality, something which could influence other people.[1]

By asking the actors to respond to the text and to various tasks of the director's invention, different ways of presenting characters and incidents are evolved in random patterns. From these the most 'forceful' are chosen, and so, 'in place of a lack of an intention, an intention appears'.[2] This kind of directing seems to avoid fixing a production according to a director's 'interpretation' or 'view', and Peter Brook's *A Midsummer Night's Dream* in the 1970 Stratford season has been hailed as a revelation by many playgoers. But the change was not so great as it sounds: the 'intention' did grow out of the rehearsals but in choosing his setting of trapezes, coiling wires and stilts, the wayward percussive music and sounds, the circus idiom and skills, Brook had made certain choices before work started. The rehearsals certainly broke new ground for many of the actors, but it can be argued that by facing them with unfamiliar tasks Brook was forcing his actors to discover what he had been looking for, instead of encouraging them to draw on their own,

[1] 'Life and Joy', an interview with Ronald Hayman, *The Times*, 29 August 1970.
[2] 'Director in Interview', with Peter Ansorge, *Plays and Players*, October 1970, pp. 18–19.

freely given creativity.[1] The production showed all along the effect of single-minded directorial decisions. For example, the speaking was slow or especially deliberate whenever the words related specifically to death or virginity, or about the actor and his art, or dream and reality. At times movement and noise obliterated speech, or made so strong a counter claim for the audience's interest that words could scarcely be followed. At other times the drama seemed to be going on inside the minds of motionless and inexpressive performers. All such effects can be made by the whole company only when they all agree to follow one instruction, and so allow a careful intensity to develop. A general impression must be given precedence over the creation of individual roles.

Time and again, the audience was forced to take the play in one comparatively simple way that owed more to a conceptual view of the play as a whole than to the obvious possibilities of Shakespeare's text. Helena and Theseus were both given kneeling positions to hold for speeches in the first Act and so were made to contradict the energy and light rhythmic variety of the writing. The Mechanicals paraded on to the stage accompanied with blaring noise that made them far more broadly comic and assertive than the words alone imply, and quite altered the textual contrast between their speeches and Helena's preceding soliloquy. Certain words were chosen for repetition, usually by a listener, and so were underlined as they are not in the text. Laughter was provided on stage with no direct cue in Shakespeare's words, and while the theatre audience remained silent. Helena's quarrel with Demetrius

[1] Two accounts have been published of rehearsals. John Kane played Puck in the production and wrote of 'Plotting with Peter' in the Royal Shakespeare Company's *Flourish*, II, 7 (1971): 'Having thus placed my head in the lion's mouth, I waited for the jaws to close.' Subsequently he found the rehearsal period both painful and stimulating, whether working on single words, alone with director in an empty studio, or in active collaboration with the other actors. He sought all the time to follow 'Peter's advice, or his advice as I understood it.' David Selbourne, the dramatist, observed rehearsals and gave his account in 'Brook's *Dream*' in *Culture and Agitation* (Action Books, 1972), pp. 13–28: 'This was a production in crisis', he starts; and he argues that the 'Director as God' had exploited the actors to obtain a 'technically brilliant, applause-winning, director-shaped commodity.'

43

was made funny by the boy falling on to the floor, the girl crawling on to his back, and he trying to crawl from underneath. Bottom was carried off to Titania's bower accompanied by large phallic gestures and cries of triumph, when the concluding words in that incident suggest delicacy and silence:

> Come, wait upon him; lead him to my bower.
> The moon, methinks, looks with a wat'ry eye;
> And when she weeps, weeps every little flower,
> Lamenting some enforced chastity.
> Tie up my love's tongue, bring him silently.
>
> (III. i. 182–6)

The roles of Hippolyta and Titania, Theseus and Oberon, were doubled without any attempt to deceive the audience, as if the actors' task was to make what likeness exists between the pairs as obvious and inescapable as possible, and to minimize the very considerable differences. Verbally certain phrases were given overwhelming importance by pauses and exaggerated enunciation, which only directorial decision could permit. One such item picked out for emphasis was 'cold . . . fruitless . . . moon' (I. i. 73), which was spoken so slowly and portentously that the incidental phrase became a posed invocation, at least an evocation, for which the pace of the action (and of the metre) had to be suspended. The actors were trying to impress what Peter Brook had chosen from among what they, themselves, had found in the carefully agitated rehearsals.

Speaking after the rehearsals were complete, Peter Brook was obviously a director committed to one particular interpretation. While he quoted the text in his own support, it is noticeable how easily he contradicted it, or misrepresented it. Now he was concerned only with what the experiments had thrown up, not only from the text but also from his own and his actors' predilections and theatrical improvisations. So in an interview, he has said that:

> Theseus and Hippolyta are trying to discover what constitutes the true union of a couple,[1]

but what he should have said is that this issue came to interest

---

[1] *Plays and Players*, op. cit., p. 19.

the actors who had the task of presenting the two characters. Nothing in the text identifies this concern, and it is quite as likely to derive from the fantasies of the experimenting and questioning actors as from the subtextual possibilities of the play. Speaking of Oberon, Brook explained the dramatic point that he had chosen to present, in the extreme terms of a 'total' love: he is

> a man taking the wife whom he loves totally and having her fucked by the crudest sex machine he can find. . . . Oberon's deliberate cool intention is to degrade Titania as a woman.

The director has here left the text far behind. First, Shakespeare's Oberon believes he is a 'creature of another sort', a fairy not a man. Second, he does not choose a 'sex machine' of any sort, but expects Titania to have more general 'hateful fantasies' (II. i. 258) and is prepared for her to 'love *and languish*' for any 'vile thing' (II. ii. 27–34). When Oberon has enchanted Titania, he still does not know what she will 'dote on' (III. ii. 3), and hearing of Bottom's transformation says, specifically, that 'This falls out better than I could devise' (l. 35). Finally, the object of devotion is not an ass, but a man with an ass's head who never says a word that suggests an intention to fuck her, crudely or otherwise. Bottom's first thought is of how to escape, his second of answering Titania's attendants with requisite courtesy. When Titania is seen 'coying' his cheeks and kissing his ears, he is irritated by an itch, feels hungry, and then announces simply – or perhaps ambiguously – that he is tired (IV. i. 1–42). The director, with his actors to help him, has discovered a concept of the play that is not represented in the play-text at all, but springs from reactions, predispositions, theatrical consciousness and fantasies of their own, and the director has used his authority to force this upon the audience's attention with elaborate business, noise, vocal reactions and climactic placing at the end of the first half of the performance.

Most critics have proclaimed a new way of staging Shakespeare after seeing Brook's production, but what seems newest is the use of rehearsals for playing with the text in order to invent business and discover an interpretation that suits his own interests and the actors with whom he is working. While this rehearsal method is said to release the potential of the text, what in fact the 'chaos' with which rehearsals began has led to is a limited, eccentric, single-minded (and rather simple-minded) interpretation – that can be expressed conceptually like any other.

4

Elizabethan Shakespeare: theatres and audiences

'The work of rehearsals', said Peter Brook, 'is looking for meaning and then making it meaningful.'[1] With designer and actors, the director becomes committed to the 'meaning' he has found and uses all his skill to make it strong and capable of exciting his audience.

In much the same way, a scholar will study the play's text as if with new eyes, with a specialized knowledge of Elizabethan rhetoric or dramatic conventions, of Elizabethan attitudes to witches, or kings, or justice and mercy; and he will then marshall an argument that will seek to influence his readers so that they see the play his way and appreciate the new meaning he has discovered. The critic will use special skills when reading a text, analysing its imagery, play-structure and 'social content', or he will compare a Shakespeare tragedy with other tragedies or with tragi-comedies, and so arrive at a new formulation of the nature and meaning of Shakespeare's play and then present it as clearly and persuasively as he can.

Both director and scholar, at the back of their minds, may acknowledge that their own meanings are only aspects of some greater meaning, and that the play will always elude their particular grasp. But director and scholar both work as if reaching towards the meaning that is right for now, the distillation of the play that speaks to himself and to his generation. It is with something of a shock that one realizes that any concern with meaning in these senses was foreign to the theatre for which Shakespeare wrote. The performances which he imagined for his plays were not the result of a search for some new and comprehensive interpretation. They were organized as little

[1] Quoted, Charles Marowitz, *'Lear* Log', *Tulane Drama Review*, viii, 2 (1963), 105.

as possible, so that individual actors were free to do as they pleased from day to day. Rather than display a finished and highly worked production in which each element contributed towards a recognized purpose, the Elizabethan theatre gave performances that changed daily, that responded to accidental stimuli and half-considered, intuitive, individual modifications. The only stable and unifying elements were the stage-space and equipment, the words of the text, the skill, art and personalities of individual actors, and the time, place and audience of the occasion. There was no director to conduct the performance, and no critic to call for a revaluation. Each day, as the play was performed, some precarious unity, some occasional coherence, would emerge from that day's special chemistry.

The word 'production' was unknown: each performance was itself. It was a theatre for discovery not for display, for happenings and unexpected conflagrations, and also for lack of fire and inefficient confusion.

Each time Shakespeare saw one of his own plays performed, he would have seen it in a new guise, modified from moment to moment by factors over which he had no control. This is so different from careful productions or scholarly research and argument that we should pause in our own response to the plays to compare our methods of staging with the Elizabethan and to inquire in more detail about the life that the texts used to have in performance and in men's imaginations. Do our methods stifle the plays?

As we have seen, knowledge of Elizabethan theatre buildings and their equipment has led in the present century to many changes in the way in which we set Shakespeare in our own theatres. An obvious next step would be to mount experiments to see whether the ways in which the Elizabethans rehearsed and ran their repertories could be adapted to our usage. But for at least two good reasons little has been done along this line. First, the major work on *The Elizabethan Stage*, which was published in four volumes in 1923 and has formed the basis for almost all subsequent research, was by E. K. Chambers, a civil servant working in the Department of Education. While he made clear where the theatres were situated, who owned them, who worked in them, what plays were performed, and so on, he gave little attention to acting or staging, to rehearsal methods or the kind of excitement that performances gave to an audience. This bias has continued in scholarly research. The second difficulty is that there is less clear evidence about how the Elizabethan actors worked and what performances were like than about other aspects of their theatre; even in more self-conscious ages these important aspects of theatre work are seldom recorded fully. But we do know something of these matters, and once certain facts about the functioning of Elizabethan theatre companies are compared with similar facts from our own theatre, some useful inferences can be drawn. The huge differences between the two theatres may be sufficient reason to explain why our theatre practice has not been influenced by this knowledge.

*   *   *

The Elizabethan theatre was fashionable and irrepressibly popular. A single acting company, without permanent subsidy except payment for work done, could operate continuously for nearly fifty years. The Head of State and his senior officers, unskilled workers, learned scholars and the innovating, rebellious young, all patronized the same plays and the same theatre companies. Clearly the success of this theatre was different from that of our own, and so were the conditions of performance.

First the staging: their audience was in the daylight and many of its members stood throughout the performance; we settle in our seats, the auditorium darkens – even in 'Elizabethan-type' buildings – and we concentrate our private attention. Beer was sold during performances in the Elizabethan theatres and one's neighbour in the audience could easily compete for attention with the actors on stage. There was no stage-lighting, no means of picking out one single figure, no atmospheric suggestion: *Hamlet* began without the murky, quiet darkness to which we are accustomed, but in broad daylight. They had no taped sound-effects. There was no scenic illusion to set tone or location: Belmont and Venice were not obviously contrasted in appearance, the one commercial and the other

49

romantic, but they were the same place with only costumes and a few properties changed. Scenes in the court and on heath and battlefield had the same background in *King Lear*. In *Othello*, Venice was basically the same as Cyprus. The action could move from the Forest of Arden to the Duke's court with no cumbersome change of set or swift change of lighting.

The difference between Elizabethan actors and our own is at least as great. Their actors actually *ran* their theatres; they were not hired by month or year, nor were they members of a company on permanent contract under a director. Ten or so actors, called the King's Men, owned their own theatre, chose the plays, paid the dramatists, and hired the 'Door Keepers'; and they took the profits. They acted in the plays with the help of 'hired men' (as the non-permanent actors were called: *not* actors), and with the help of boys. They worked a repertory system so that, around the year 1600, one company could have had thirty or so plays in production available for performance at any one time. We know that a single company, in 1594, put on fifteen entirely new plays within six months, as well as many revivals. Early in 1613, the King's Men presented 'fourteen several plays' at court, and a little later the same season repeated two of them and added four more titles. The programme was always changing so that a run of two or three days would be exceptional. Moreover plays were kept in the repertoire for ten, fifteen or twenty years. These companies acted not only in their own theatres but also at court, in great houses and in universities. Their actors must have worked long and hard, and they must have been very adaptable and alert. They were on their own, too, for there was no dramatic criticism to guide them: the few accounts of their performance that have survived are private and personal.

Generally in the theatre today, there are two ideals of acting: the stars and the *ensembles*; prestige productions for special occasions on the one hand, and established companies or new groups and communes on the other. What would happen if the artistic control of a theatre was put in the hands of ten experienced actors? Actors are not good administrators, it will be argued: but is this always or necessarily so? Might not the actor's attitude to his art and his job change if he knew that

this responsibility would be his? And might not this responsibility deepen and extend the scope of his art? The Elizabethan
actors managed theatres.

Today actors do not have to 'hold' their audiences single-
handed. The director has seen to it that lighting, grouping,
mass movements, stage-business, sustained pauses, rhythms,
scenery and costume all focus attention where he wants it. The
audience in the dark has its gaze held by the brightly or subtly
lit stage. Music or sound-effects support entrances and exits,
and can provide irresistible rhythmic control. What was it like
when actors performed with the house lights up? They probably
worked less subtly, and must have been more dominating, outgoing, clear, physical. They must have been remarkable and
outstanding. They must have acted without pause in order to
sustain any illusion of reality or sufficient continuity. They
would have been inwardly aware all the time that they could
lose their audience, and they could never have relied on the
overwhelming established reality of scenery or atmospheric
lighting and sound. When an actor stepped on to the stage, the
audience would not have been conditioned to *take in* whatever
he offered; rather the actor must have worked to *take over* the
audience.

Today, actors work for weeks or months in rehearsal – we
are always being told that longer time is required – work under
a director in order to fix the details of each production. Supernumeraries are given elaborate movements and carefully
differentiated involvement; stage-business is devised that could
be dangerous without well-drilled control; everyone co-operates
towards a single, defined purpose which is commonly decided
upon long before rehearsals begin. There are preview performances and adjustments before the production is completed, each
effect carefully chosen, developed and controlled; and then
the production is shown to the public sometimes by itself, sometimes taking its turn with three or four other plays that have
already been produced in equal detail. The play can then 'run'
smoothly on successive nights, and the actor can subtly modify
what he is doing, within clear limits, for the next few months or,
perhaps, a year or two. Is this the best way to produce a play?
It is almost universal practice today, but for the Elizabethans,

with no 'runs' and thirty plays in a single repertoire, such proceedings would have been impossible and unthinkable.

To follow Elizabethan practice in rehearsal, production and repertoire, would mean forgoing all that is valued most highly in our productions; new interpretations of the plays, and definitive and unified performance. Instead of a director, there would be a 'book keeper', as the Elizabethans called their functionary who combined the jobs of prompter and stage-manager. The title is significant: this man held the 'book', and so anchored performances, ensuring that properties were ready and actors called as required by the play-text. He was not an important member of the company, for the name of none of them has survived in the records. In addition, an author might give what were called 'instructions' to the players. But with so many plays in repertoire little time could be allotted for a new production, still less to a play being revived, for one perform-ance or two, after the lapse of some months. Clearly nothing at all subtle or elaborate in the way of business, movement, inflection or pause could have been 'fixed', and each perform-ance must have had an element of uncertainty. If the dramatist was present and tried to influence matters, he must have chosen only the most salient points for attention, or given most of his 'instructions' in general terms; an actor could not take in much more than this for a routine one-night performance of one play among many. No one on stage could have been quite sure where or how he was to be confronted by his fellow actors. Tempo, rhythm, grouping, business must have altered from day to day. His resource, in this uncertainty, must have been his own study of his part, often in private, and his ability to adapt to the play as it was played on each individual occasion.

This way of working is nicely illustrated by the practice in Elizabethan theatres of not giving the actor the text of the play in which he was to perform, but only his own part, written out with the brief verbal cues on which he had to speak. He must have listened hard during performance, and it was up to him, while performing on stage in front of an audience, to see and communicate the precise relevance of his part to the dramatic reality as a whole, as that reality was created, moment by moment, in unfixed, unrepeatable detail.

However precarious this way of working may seem to us, the Elizabethans have left no complaint, except of the clown who spoke more than was set down for him – and it was the dramatist who seems to have been most offended at this. I can only suppose that the actor must have overcome his nervousness – which is so much a part of his art, even in our own highly controlled productions – by ensuring that he knew his cues and words unshakably and, still more, by creating a firm, unvarying inner-reality of character and a complete physical embodiment. Only from such a base would he be free and able to improvise the handling of so much verbal detail in so changeable a context. He may well have had familiar routines, clichés perhaps, on which he could rely, and a few very simple and essential moves or groupings were probably agreed upon beforehand in the short group rehearsals that were available. But exactly how he should play would depend on the conditions of each performance, the exact nature of his own private preparation for that occasion, and on the performances of the other actors. Because almost nothing besides the words was 'fixed', as we say, his contribution could and would change from day to day, according to his state of mind and feeling, his reactions to life and events outside the theatre. Tempo would change; different parts of his role would be pointed according to his own experience of living and his own fantasies, and its impression be strengthened in response to his growing acquaintance with the play and with his fellow actors. He would be influenced, too, by his audience, which was not separated from him by darkness and could support or ignore him according to their changing concerns, the time of year, or the political climate. Every play, despite the elaborate words which were its controlling element, must have been precarious in performance, and every performance must have been different from another.

There must have been a large element of risk in theatre-going. Instead of a well-oiled machine, a performance was more like a football match, in that the actors' skill was always wholly on trial: the quality of play was part of the play. It was a 'happening' in that, except for the words spoken, it was free, moment by moment. Discovery was possible; and disappointment too. An Elizabethan performance must have been like a thoroughly committed rehearsal in our theatre; and sometimes – perhaps often – the audience was able to share the excitement we know when a rehearsal suddenly goes right, that transfigures routine work into surprising and exhilarating creation, the consuming and all-embracing excitement which the public today never witnesses, and never shares.

Elizabethan performances must have been far simpler visually. There was no lighting plot, with fixed points of emphasis and dramatic cross-lighting. Carefully timed entrances and exits, complicated pieces of special business with sword or costume or furniture, controlled pauses and elaborate crescendoes were outside their range of activity. The number of supernumeraries used to fill out a scene and control rhythm and visual focus could not have been very large, or their activities and interplay with the main characters complicated.

It is symptomatic of the Elizabethan approach to stage-craft that they did not ask 'how are we going to set this play?' but, rather, 'how are we going to put it on the stage?' This turn of phrase is characteristic: if this were 'played upon the stage', said Shakespeare in *Twelfth Night*, or 'upon this narrow floor', said Thomas Dekker.[1] George Chapman did not speak of 'putting on a play' as we do, but of actions 'brought upon stages'.[2] We speak of Winston Churchill or Lenin being put *into* a play, or of writing a play *about* him; but Thomas Nashe, the Elizabethan novelist and playwright, said that 'brave Talbot' was made to 'triumph again on the stage'.[3] Their characters were not 'in a play', but 'on a stage'; they were at once more immediate, individual, and exposed. Supposing that *King Lear* were 'set upon a stage', forgetting scenery and carefully drilled production support, and placing the audience in the same clear light, what might be seen? We would lose impressions of space, of particular place, of everyday physical background and behaviour. The actor would be a man among other men, in space, seeking a performance controlled by the words and based in his own imaginative conception and physical creation of his role. He could not pause for long without losing

[1] *The Whore of Babylon* (1604), Prologue.
[2] *The Revenge of Bussy D' Ambois* (1608), I. i.
[3] *Pierce Penniless* (1592); ed. S. Wells (1964), pp. 64–5.

hold of his audience who sat in judgement on him and in immediate contact, sharing the same light, the same accidental distractions and an awareness of the always-changing present moment. Movement would have to be lively and physical performance strong. It sounds frightening for the actors, but the Elizabethans flourished under these conditions; and so did their dramatists, and their audiences.

A further consequence of the lessening of control would be the freeing of the audience, as well as the actor. Today an audience's response is guided fairly precisely. The stage can be darkened to avoid laughter, a silence insisted upon so that the following words seem of overwhelming importance, a rhythmic uneasiness can be prepared so that a few clear, settled movements that follow are brought into unavoidable prominence. But audiences sitting or standing in broad daylight feel free to withdraw attention and to criticize by talk between themselves. When their attention is gained, it will be freely given and without reserve. Such attention can be penetrating and wholly exciting. Moreover the individual members of an audience are in contact with each other so that they may share, and help to build, a common response. Elizabethan theatre-going must have had the strength of corporate actions, individually discovered and freely given.

The theatre was an arena for human action and the audience's discovery, as at the moment of performance the drama came alive as never before: it was not a show-case for display. Such a limitation of dramatic effect was not puritanical or restrictive: speech, breathing, physical action and reaction, rhythm, fluid groupings and the dynamics of movement, smiles, tears, sweat, and subtle changes of face and eyes, all provided variety and excitement. The audience was not placed to receive what was selected and 'blown up' for their attention, but from a position of close contact each member was free to explore and almost share a living image which was being created by the actors with all their powers. This was a man-sized theatre: infinite in faculties, in form and meaning, express and admirable; in action and apprehension alive. The human drama was like a piece of sculpture in that it required active exploration and was variably meaningful according to the point of approach and the conditions of viewing. It was ever changing itself, for ever being created afresh.

*   *   *

Such a theatre is not wholly without modern parallels, but they all stop short of Elizabethan practice. We know perhaps enough from our own experience to gain some idea of how Shakespeare's plays were performed and received.

Small companies touring schools with the simplest equipment are perhaps closest. Playing in the ordinary classrooms, in contact with unpredictable and volatile audiences that sit in the same light, these actors become devoted to their tasks and many of them never go back to the adult theatres. Perhaps the children's enthusiasm is largely responsible for this, but the form of production must also affect their choice. Cabaret, agit-prop and street-theatre experience is also indicative of some of the artistic possibilities for the 'men set upon a stage'. The Bread and Puppet Theatre in the United States has cut free from directorial handling of movement and speech and so responds to the audience it encounters in its own surroundings. It offers a challenging 'open' form of theatre, but it has not adopted Elizabethan attitudes to rehearsals and Elizabethan use of complicated texts, large repertoires, raised and fixed stages, and it is not free from domination by one directorial command. Ed Berman's Inter-Action company in London offers another example, but its street theatre is conceived on guerrilla-like scale, and its indoor theatre is clearly under the charge of a director who supplies both guidance in detail and overall strategy.

None of these companies can give a full idea of Shakespeare's plays in performance before an Elizabethan audience. Perhaps occasional occurrences in more traditional theatres can get as close for a brief moment. For example, during a dress rehearsal of *King Lear* at Stratford-upon-Avon with Paul Scofield in the name part, the auditorium was empty except for members of the theatre staff and a photographer with his camera:

In the Hunting Scene (I. iv), where Lear becomes more and more riled by Goneril's discourtesies, Scofield seemed more agitated than usual. After overturning the table and ordering his knights to horse, Lear comes downstage and proceeds to intone one of those blood-curdling Shakespearian curses which freeze the blood. . . . In the middle of the speech, Scofield crossed downstage to the apron and hurled his hunting-cloak at the photographer whose camera had been clicking an accompaniment to Lear's speeches. 'Please get that thing away from here,' he growled in the voice of the furious Lear, and then immediately continued to berate Goneril. One could almost hear the entire auditorium catch its breath. John Goodwin, the press representative, said: 'I suddenly felt myself sweat. It was a horrifying sensation.' It occurred to me afterwards that this is precisely what the production was lacking: moments so charged and taut that one's insides suddenly ground to a stop. . . .[1]

There is a power in surprise, even if not calculated; there is an immediacy that comes if the audience is suddenly fixed or contacted, finding itself at one with a creature of furious power. In a scene where all the words are Shakespeare's and where the actions are carefully rehearsed and fixed, this fire never catches. But I think it might in a freer, more Elizabethan performance when an actor caught a new reality in the ever-changing performance and achieved its expression from his position of prepared, inner power. As Scofield brought Lear's voice to attack the photographer, he could use all his physical and imaginative preparation to create a new thrust of action and temperament.

In a television programme Sir Alec Guinness has told how Sir Tyrone Guthrie got the idea of abandoning a picture-frame theatre and reverting to the Elizabethan thrust stage. He was taking his Old Vic production of *Hamlet* to Elsinore in 1937, to play in the castle court-yard. But in the afternoon thick rain drove over the countryside and continued unceasingly. At five-thirty it was decided to move to the ballroom of the hotel near by. Gilt chairs were put in a horseshoe around the acting area, and the audience had to accommodate itself as best it could. Lighting had to be unvaried, and none of the actors was quite sure where he had to enter. But in these makeshift

---

[1] '*Lear* Log', op. cit., pp. 116–17.

conditions the production caught fire as never before. From this Guthrie deduced that he must move to a thrust stage theatre, and after nearly two decades the Festival Theatre at Stratford, Ontario, was built. But he may have missed another deduction from that night's excitement: that Shakespeare's plays work when a production is not fixed. If the audience is to be involved, if the actors are to create for each audience, each night, and if the action, characters, spectacle, themes and the whole drama are to lay open, exposed for exploration, then we must not allow actors to 'fix' everything that happens.

When Sir John Gielgud was playing Richard II for the last time for a British Council tour to Bulawayo, he called his friends one morning to a makeshift rehearsal at Her Majesty's Theatre in the Haymarket. Again there was no careful lighting plot, there were no costumes; not much was fixed, ready for the show. There was no scenery; the actors were still uncertain of their roles. And again the play was a great success; those that were there have never forgotten it. So struck was Gielgud, who had performed much of the play in his dressing-gown, that when he was asked to direct Richard Burton on Broadway as Hamlet, he tried to repeat the excitement. This time he did not catch the thrust stage idea – Her Majesty's has a good nineteenth-century picture-frame stage, a large one – but like Guthrie he did not imagine that the impromptu, the carefully prepared but free and open rendering, had done the trick. Rather than see that, he believed that it was the rehearsal costumes that had worked the magic. Consequently Burton wore a carefully chosen rehearsal costume for Broadway, and so did everyone else. But the production was fixed in every other way, and was designed to 'run' for long enough to recoup the heavy expenditure: and the magic had departed.

The Royal Shakespeare Theatre-Go-Round travelling productions often work in halls unadapted to theatre performances, taking only a very rudimentary stage set. While the company is well rehearsed and the production nicely geared to one interpretation of the play they are performing, the staging is always a more or less makeshift compromise. For some critics, like Gareth Lloyd-Evans writing in *The Guardian*, this gains something of Elizabethan conditions:

The Siege of Harfleur and the battle of Agincourt took place on a night of waterfalling rain at Stroud, Gloucestershire. The Royal Shakespeare company, true to its policy of making critics journey for their pleasures, had summoned us to an outback Theatre-go-round production of 'Henry V' at the improbably named Subscription Rooms. It was well worth it. Rarely have I seen Shakespeare's apologetic words about cramming wooden O's and making do with a few foils so revealed for what they are – a trick. With a tiny cast, loud bangs, smoke, lights, activity, and sensitivity, this unfashionably patriotic play was superbly done. It made the idea of joining that lot at Calais absolutely daft.

John Barton, the director, used no tricks (though he had some hefty cutting). It was straight down the track, full of the slog of war, the glory of speechifying, the thrill of romance and adventure. Michael Williams's Henry had poise and fire. Polly James, doubling as Katherine and that doomed battlefield boy (Falstaff's natural son?) had, for the first, wit, zest, and passion, and, for the second, a moving gamin quality. Unsung names have stuck in my memory. David Calder as a powerful Chorus, Bernard Lloyd as a shrewd really Welsh Flewellyn, Marion Lines making a true sexy officious character out of Katherine's maid, Morgan Sheppard's Pistol and Denis Holmes's Constable of France. Well done, the RSC.

But all this critical gallivanting prompts a thought. If, in appalling conditions and deprived of the chance to muck about with Shakespeare, they can pull off such wonderful stuff, and get such a reception, why does the RSC so frequently and expensively fool about with Shakespeare in its home base? This production was the nearest to a Globe Theatre presentation, I suppose I've seen, and it worked superbly without gimmickry.[1]

Makeshift conditions often correspond in some particulars to the ways of Elizabethan theatres, but they do not put the clock back or give more than a glimpse of what Shakespeare's audience witnessed in the theatre. This must remain unknown and all that we can try to do is to consider how what we know both of the Elizabethan theatre and our own can help us respond to the texts for ourselves, and perhaps to initiate experiments in theatre production.

[1] *The Guardian*, 21 June 1971.

5

Original Shakespeare: the text and its opportunities

Everyone knows how the scholar's knowledge about Elizabethan theatre buildings has influenced our staging of Shakespeare. No longer do designers contrive a separate scenic background for each scene, but keep the action moving continuously on an open stage, often backed by some structure resembling the tiring-house façade that has been made familiar in reconstructions of the Globe Playhouse. By visualizing the action on an Elizabethan stage, critics have revalued Shakespeare's achievement in play construction and have become keenly aware that the rules of a well-shaped modern play are inapplicable to his art. In the same way, knowledge about Elizabethan psychology, society, politics, religion and life has modified our reading of the plays, and sometimes has influenced theatre productions in details of characterization, staging and interpretation. With such precedents before us, we may ask whether our response to the plays should be modified in any way by an understanding of Elizabethan conditions of repertoire, theatre management, rehearsal and production.

Usually the plays are studied as material to be interpreted in terms of theme and meaning, and in the theatre they are treated as complicated scores that have to be simplified, strengthened and given a fixed and unified production – a processing, so that they may speak to the present age in its own terms. But these reactions are quite foreign to the Elizabethan age and possibly hostile to an appreciation of the inherent dramatic qualities of the plays. Could we see them, as Shakespeare and his contemporaries did, as the source of an infinite number of encounters between human beings set upon a stage, none valid beyond the unique moment of performance and all more potent in suggestion than in clear statement and developed achievement?

Viewed in this way, the words of a text could never be mistaken for the whole content of a play. Our study would be to seek out the range of possible realizations that the words have been, and may be, given. There would be little point in trying to pin down a single meaning for any speech; each possible meaning would be envisaged in its context of space, time, sound and physical embodiment. We would remember that Shakespeare himself must have been constantly surprised at his plays in performance, as the exciting and complex words became part of the actors' performance on any particular day. The changing limitations of time, place, stage and theatre equipment, the accidents of casting, memory, varying preparation and motivation, unfixed stage-business and interaction between the actors, and the unforeseeable excitement of each individual audience who received and responded to the play, would all combine in ever-fresh arrangements to make each performance unique, and in its own terms consistent. It is the ability of the text to support and control this range of performances that we should try to study. A search for a text's variable potential in theatrical realization is a far different task from an attempt to express its meanings or to pluck out the heart of its mystery.

In staging the plays an attempt to accommodate Elizabethan attitudes would cut right across modern repertory systems or the long run, the director's control of staging and performance, and, I suspect, the whole managerial and financial basis of production. A new kind of audience would also be required. But short of such a radical change, there might be some adaptation of our present methods, to give greater flexibility to actors and to avoid rigorous unification according to meanings that have been too simply or too intellectually defined. Such compromises might be rewarding because the plays were designed for free, active and explorative performances, in the same way as a flexible Elizabethan-type setting allows their basic dramatic structure to speak without impediment.

Paradoxically a return to Elizabethan presentation and reception would not entail museum-type productions or an attempt to reconstruct an Elizabethan response – both of which seem to me to be impossible labour. The essential element of this Elizabethan method would be the freedom of both stage presentation and study to respond to the new conditions that history has brought about, to win back the proper allowance for the text to adapt, as it was designed to adapt, to the new actors, theatres, audiences and readers of this present day.

*   *   *

The many different and conflicting interpretations that each of Shakespeare's major characters has been given on stage and in scholarly study, each convincing in its own context, are the most obvious indication of the chameleon qualities of Shakespeare's text. His words lie open to almost any interpretation. So Hamlet the Prince of Denmark is an active and highly-charged revenger or an intellectual poisoned by self-doubt and disappointed love. Or he is a poet, taking refuge from a harsh world in his own liberating mind. In recent years we have seen David Warner's apathetic Hamlet, Alan Bates's imprisoned Hamlet, Ian McKellen's isolated, emotional idealistic and intelligent Hamlet; there have been honest Hamlets, crippled, adolescent, beautiful, ugly Hamlets; short, tall, revolutionary and contemporary Hamlets. Shylocks have been noble and wronged, mercenary and cruel, fantastic and devilish. Prosperos have been powerful and loving or bewildered and cruel. Whole plays have been unlocked by different keys, so that *Julius Caesar* centres on the Emperor and his heir, or on Brutus, or on Cassius, or on Antony and the mob of citizens. *Measure for Measure* can speak confidently for Christian virtues or show the weakness of all assumed authority, or the play can be presented as a study of repression in which only sex and laughter can bring delight. Scholars have been equally prolific in contrasting arguments, so that Shakespeare has been Catholic and Protestant, agnostic, existentialist and pragmatist, sophist and deliberate philosophizer.

But to understand the ways in which Shakespeare wrote his plays so that they remain open to various interpretations at any moment in performance we must look more closely at the texts. From the very start of a play, in the actors' first appearances, the dialogue gives free scope. For example, when in *Antony and Cleopatra* the protagonists enter, they say:

CLEOPATRA: If it be love indeed, tell me how much.
ANTONY: There's beggary in the love that can be reckon'd.
CLEOPATRA: I'll set a bourn how far to be belov'd.
ANTONY: Then must thou needs find out new heaven, new earth.

(I. i. 14–17)

Perhaps the most obvious way for the actors to perform these lines is to speak the first two slowly and rapturously, the third half teasingly, and the fourth with new rapture and fantasy. But the first line could be spoken teasingly, tauntingly, as the lovers refuse an embrace; the tempo would then be much quicker and Antony's two lines might be either earnest entreaty or incredulous delight. Or, yet differently, Cleopatra could speak with instinctive doubt, and Antony give light and mocking answers. Or Cleopatra could enjoy the pretence of fear, and Antony either play her game or answer from self-righteous belief in his own fantasy of love. The four lines can go slow or fast, skippingly or nervously; they can be intimacies overheard, or they can be a public show that covers up their inward content, or anxiety, or appetite. Perhaps the surest indication of how Shakespeare imagined that they would be spoken lies in the metre, which gives Antony the irregularities, the larger hint of nervousness; but then in his choice of words he seems the more confident, and if we try to judge Shakespeare's intentions in this way we shall again be setting the word against the word in endless variations. In fact many renderings can find strength in the way the passage is written and theatre history shows that all the interpretations that have been suggested here, and others, have worked upon occasion, according to the actors' talents and intentions, and a director's purpose. Other plays with comparably variable openings to the major roles include *Twelfth Night, Hamlet, Macbeth* and *Lear*.

Shakespeare's intention to offer this freedom seems most certain when he has placed a simple-seeming line so crucially that it is a fulcrum capable of leading an actor in several exclusively opposing directions, according to the way in which he speaks it. Many of these have become famous, for audiences have recognized their power. For example, when Hal pretends to be his father, the king, in *Henry IV, Part One*, and answers the rhetoric of Falstaff who speaks in his person, he uses only four simple words:

> FALSTAFF: . . . but, for sweet Jack Falstaff, kind Jack Falstaff, true Jack Falstaff, valiant Jack Falstaff – and therefore more valiant, being, as he is, old Jack Falstaff – banish not him thy Harry's company, banish not him thy Harry's company. Banish plump Jack, and banish all the world.
> PRINCE: I do, I will. (II. iv. 459–64)

At this point, a knocking is heard on the door, and news comes from the real court. Hal can say 'I do' solemnly, as if he has become another person, his father, almost against his own intention; and then 'I will' can follow as a return to his own person who still compromises with the time and his royal responsibilities. Or 'I do' can be said with cold calculation, revealing the astute mind of the young prince who is using his friends as a cover for his own purposes; and 'I will' can be a kind of apology, so that the play-acting of the reprobate son can continue without disrupting embarrassment. Or both parts of Hal's short answer can be accompanied with actorish gestures, as if he still enjoys the pretended reality and still mocks his father, unconscious of any deeper demands; such a Hal will hold back from fuller knowledge of himself until after the death of Hotspur when his own father is dying, or when Falstaff kneels before him in his own person and he himself wears the crown. In any of these ways, the line is powerful, the knocking on the door breaking off the confrontation without taking away from the point the actor chooses to make in this brief, variable and effective summation.

Further examples of fulcrum lines are Beatrice's 'Kill Claudio' in *Much Ado About Nothing* (IV. i. 287), which as a passionate, instinctive response or as a challenging act of intelligence, brings Benedick suddenly to a new seriousness, and gives him an almost equally precarious response: 'Ha! not for the wide world.' In the first scene of *Othello*, Iago talks with Roderigo about service, promotion, the Moor and Cassio, and concludes with 'I am not what I am' (l. 66). This can be said smiling straight in Roderigo's face, and so show Iago's delight in baffling his dupe. Or it can be said coldly, as a warning to Roderigo, or as an avoidance of further talk which allows Iago a moment of inner resolve and committal to the path of deceit and murder. Or the six simple words can be said as a delighted soliloquy, showing Iago's confidence in his own powers, or in his independence. Or it can be said to the audience and so represent a warning that Iago gives to the world, either solemnly or in mockery. Not only is the ambivalent line placed at the conclusion of Iago's speech, but Roderigo is given no reply, like those which have hitherto shown him to be following Iago's thought; now Roderigo changes the subject, and Iago then turns to immediate action. The few words are an unmistakable opportunity for the actor to impress the audience with his own reading of the part, to take the spotlight of attention with a line that can be used as a keystone for many different characterizations.

Perhaps the most crucially placed of such simple lines are those in *Lear* when the king dies with Cordelia in his arms:

> Do you see this? Look on her. Look, her lips.
> Look there, look there! (V. iii. 310–11)

Is Lear showing the onlookers that there is 'no breath at all', so that he dies in outraged despair? Or does he die believing that there is a sign of life, that something stirs within the beloved daughter whose life could redeem all sorrow? If he dies in hope, how far does that transform him? Is it a pathetic flicker or a glow that seems to grow in strength as Lear enters another world of satisfied imagination? If the end is loss, how bitter is the hatred and how great the need for corroboration? Does Lear gain strength through knowledge of the facts? And whether he dies in hope or despair, what pain does he feel – 'Pray you undo this button', probably means that at least he is fighting for breath – and how far does that pain seem to become irrelevant to his concern for Cordelia, or for his assembled friends, or for true knowledge of his state? The end of *King Lear* can hardly be other than a moving experience, but the last view of the king himself can suggest a wide range of reactions. In a new production there is always doubt of the outcome of the tragedy in terms of the protagonist's victory or defeat at the moment of death. Shakespeare seems to have left the options open with deliberate intent.

Indeed the endings of his plays provide more examples than elsewhere of the players' need to choose among many possible interpretations. Or, to put this the other way about, the endings allow the players opportunity to make their own individual mark in their roles, at the moment when it can stay most securely in the minds of their audience. Act V of *Twelfth Night* is especially rich in this way. When Sebastian enters to the assembled company, which includes his twin Viola who is dressed exactly like him, the dialogue is comparatively simple:

SEBASTIAN: Antonio, O my dear Antonio!
　　　　　　How have the hours rack'd and tortur'd me
　　　　　　Since I have lost thee!
ANTONIO: Sebastian are you?
SEBASTIAN: 　　　　　　　　　Fear'st thou that, Antonio?
ANTONIO: How have you made division of yourself?
　　　　　An apple cleft in two is not more twin
　　　　　Than these two creatures. Which is Sebastian?
　　　　　　　　　　　　　　　　　(V. i. 210–16)

The incomplete verse-line suggests a pause before Antonio speaks, and this can serve either to build up a comic effect or to enable Antonio to establish a rapt amazement that could silence laughter – in this case Sebastian can start the laughter with his reply. In whatever way this interchange is played, it will affect the next speech, which is Olivia's 'Most wonderful!' These two words are capable of many interpretations, from rapt or thankful astonishment, through hesitation and doubt, or even fear, to open coquettishness. In the Royal Shakespeare Theatre's production of 1960, these words held up the action for an appreciable time as the audience, according to the critic of *The Scotsman*, went 'into fits of laughter: it was as if Miss Barnet [as Olivia] was welcoming the prospect of two husbands.'

Less than sixty lines later, Malvolio leaves the stage after a conspicuous silence which has been intensified by Feste, Fabian and Olivia all speaking of him or to him. Yet Shakespeare has given Malvolio only one sentence to speak as he leaves: 'I'll be reveng'd on the whole pack of you' (l. 364): these nine words are sufficient to crown many enterprising and imaginative performances; and they have so filled the minds of audiences that they seem an effective close to the whole play. Malvolio can seem to gather the shreds of dignity about him again, or he can seem foolishly or pathetically blind to reality. The audience may laugh or catch its breath. When Henry Irving played the part, he brought

> into most powerful relief the deeper nature of the 'madly used' steward himself, as an Italian who can be, when fully roused by injustice, as vindictive as Shylock . . . and as implacable as Othello. . . . He does not slink from the stage a baffled and gulled simpleton. . . . 'I'll be revenged on the whole pack of you' he screams, rather than exclaims, as he rushes from the stage. When an Italian by the name of Mal-voglio vows that he will take vengeance on his enemies, it is clear that he means mischief. Olivia begins to be frightened. . . .[1]

In contrast, John Gielgud's 'sere and yellow Malvolio, Puritan to the core', left the stage with cold deliberation and 'snarled his spiteful exit'.[2] Laurence Olivier turned the words into the natural, pained cry of a man who is ruined. who 'refuses to see himself as others see him'.[3] Sometimes in this last scene it is silence which offers the actor greatest choice for concluding his performance, as when Sir Toby enters having been soundly cudgelled by Sebastian for his rudeness. This is the knight's only appearance in Act V and, unusually, he has few words. He first speaks when Orsino puts two questions to him, and these he brushes aside and turns instead to the fool who is now accompanying him. Is he accepting removal from polite society, or trying to behave as if it did not exist? Beneath his subsequent silence, when all eyes are directed towards him,

[1] *Illustrated London News*, 12 July 1884.
[2] *The Observer*, 11 January, 1931.
[3] *Shakespeare: a celebration*, ed. T. J. B. Spencer (1964), pp. 81–2.

anger or self-reproach can be suggested; or, in his strutting across the stage and concern for his wound, he may be seen as the undefeatable clown, the comic whose world is at his own command so long as he continues in this role. When Olivia speaks, it is about Sir Toby, and not to him; she seems to feel herself separated from him, or unable to communicate with such a confirmed egotist. If Feste and Fabian busy themselves in getting Sir Toby to bed, as Olivia has directed, Sir Andrew is then free to make a slower exit and so draw the last attention to himself without speaking a single word. Actors have used this opportunity in many ways: Sir Andrew may weep, or he may panic, or he can show a growing discernment, or make a last attempt to catch Olivia's attention – whatever seems appropriate to the performance as a whole.

The entry of the Priest in the last scene of *Twelfth Night* introduces new rhythms and a firm, untroubled and even other-worldly voice as he attests to Olivia's marriage. He may leave the stage soon after he has given evidence, but there is no certain indication that he should do so. If he remains in view of the audience, he can continue to serve silently as a reminder of solemn vows, while the rest of the world runs topsy-turvy: Sir Andrew can apply to him for aid, with 'for the love of God, your help!' (l. 170); Malvolio can ask for confirmation that he had been visited in prison (l. 329); Feste can imitate his voice a second time (at l. 359), and Orsino can appeal to him for a 'solemn combination . . . of our dear souls' (ll. 369–70). Clearly there is considerable dramatic potential in the Priest's presence on stage, but Shakespeare did not draw unmistakably upon it. If the Priest is the last to leave the stage before Feste takes attention with his concluding song – and social decorum could well allow for this – he would be a reminder of immortality alongside the perpetual fool who had earlier imitated him and his counsel. Conversely, the Priest could leave the stage first at the end of the comedy, so that it would be Antonio, the steadfast lover who must now relinquish Sebastian, who is seen last at the moment when the fool begins to preside over the end of the comedy.

Certainly Viola's last contribution to the comedy is a silent one, as she responds to Orsino's concluding words:

> Cesario, come;
> For so you shall be while you are a man;
> But when in other habits you are seen,
> Orsino's mistress, and his fancy's queen.

Does she come to him gaily or thoughtfully? Do they leave slowly or quickly? Do they touch, or do they kiss, or do they consciously and gravely delay all intimacy until 'golden time convents'? They may strive to appear more assured of themselves than they are in reality at this giddy minute so soon after mistakes, disguises, confidences and fears have all been revealed. Shakespeare's words require that Viola moves towards Orsino before leaving the stage so that all attention is upon her; but the manner of her movement and of the *exeunt* that follows have been left open for the actors' choice. The scene and the comedy can conclude with a sensitive response to however much of mutual concern has been expressed in the course of each performance; the conclusion has to be 'played by ear', as actors say.

*　　*　　*

At significant crises of the plays Shakespeare has sometimes arranged that physical bearing or some piece of stage-business easily dominates all other impressions, and so he has allowed the drama to respond to the physique, temperament and intention of the actor and to the excitement of the drama as it develops in each particular performance.

There are several examples of these open opportunities in *Othello*. When the Moor falls insensible to the ground in a fit, Iago is left in charge of the great hulk. His words are:

> Work on,
> My medicine work. Thus credulous fools are caught;
> And many worthy and chaste dames even thus,
> All guiltless, meet reproach.　　　　　(IV. i. 44–7)

but the sight of the new lieutenant standing over the general catches the eye. Iago can mark his triumph quietly, or with mocking laughter; some Iagos strike or kick Othello, or spit or stand upon him. The speed with which Iago tries to awaken his victim is also significant theatrically: a quiet, cold moment's pause, or a movement onwards with quick appetite for the next round in their contest, can mark the actor's individual feel for the character he is creating.

In the following scene, the actor of Othello can take an opportunity to suggest that the Moor is still capable of believing Desdemona to be honest, and could mark this with an embrace. He is denouncing his wife:

OTHELLO:	Impudent strumpet!
DESDEMONA:	By heaven, you do me wrong.
OTHELLO:	Are not you a strumpet?
DESDEMONA:	No, as I am a Christian.
	If to preserve this vessel for my lord
	From any other foul unlawful touch
	Be not to be a strumpet, I am none.
OTHELLO:	What, not a whore?
DESDEMONA:	No, as I shall be sav'd.
OTHELLO:	Is't possible?
DESDEMONA:	O, heaven forgive us!
OTHELLO:	I cry you mercy, then.
	I took you for that cunning whore of Venice. . . .

(IV. ii. 82–90)

This can be played as if Othello never, for an instant, takes Desdemona's words for truth. But the very short verse-line 'Is't possible?' suggests a pause in which belief could come flooding back: they can embrace, and the 'us' of Desdemona's next speech ('O, heaven forgive us!') will seem particularly meaningful if this is so. If they do embrace, it can only be until Othello's contact with the body his imagination has defiled leads to recoil, and he starts away with sarcasm, cruelty and renewed intent to bring about the destruction of his bride and of everything to do with her. On the other hand 'Is't possible' can be brutally ironic, and the pause help the actor to register by his bearing the isolation of Othello as he purposes revenge; perhaps Desdemona weeps, or falls back, away from her husband, no longer able to plead. Or the words can be a cue for Othello to gaze upwards, or out and beyond the figure kneeling before him, as if he contemplates his fate and the prophecy of the sybil who had woven the handkerchief; so he might seem to see himself as the plaything of the gods. This physical enactment would be equally dominating, and would make particular sense of Othello's reference to the 'gate of hell' that follows immediately afterwards, with its implication of eternal damnation.

Perhaps the most notable opportunity in this play for an actor to create his own physical response is at the very end, when Iago is addressed by Lodovico:

> O Spartan dog,
> More fell than anguish, hunger, or the sea!
> Look on the tragic loading of this bed.
> This is thy work. (V. ii. 364–7)

Some reaction from Iago is inevitable here, for even if he remains inscrutable, the refusal of a more open response will be marked by the audience once Lodovico has so drawn attention to him. Some Iagos take an initiative earlier and laugh as Cassio concludes his immediately preceding speech:

> This did I fear, but thought he had no weapon;
> For he was great of heart.

Other Iagos wait to reveal their full response until Lodovico has left the stage and they are due to follow; so they can make their last effect speak for themselves alone, as if their hatred of the world and perhaps of themselves outlasts the tragic loading of the bed, which has now been hidden from sight. Many reports testify to the effectiveness of Iago's last, wordless contribution to the play and show that the focus Shakespeare has brought to bear upon this silent figure is capable of registering the finest, most precise effects. For example, *The Sunday Times* said of Richard Burton's Iago at the Old Vic, London, in 1956, that he was:

> betrayed only by his cold eyes, which command the scene at last, when defeated, bound and bleeding, he strikes across the stage at Othello's corpse a long yellow glare of triumph.

Usually the judgement of the actor in such open opportunities must reckon with more than his own characterization, for the truth and power of whatever is done depends on those acting with him. There is, indeed, an element of contest or mutual exploration in every production of a Shakespeare play. Many of the crucial scenes are encounters between two or three characters in which the balance of power shifts from one side to another, or where different elements in the situation are revealed successively and, as it were, tested for strength. Although the text often directs who it is that is left in possession or who breaks off the contest, the relative effectiveness of each party depends on precisely how the encounter has been played: who withdraws attention first, who avoids a straight look or who scarcely registers a blow, who speaks quickly and who slowly, and whether speed speaks for fear or confidence. Shakespeare has frequently provided moments where the stillness of direct and silent confrontation seems to be required, as at a fulcrum point, and here the exact bearing and look of the contestants can tip the balance of power or trust. This will seldom mean that the action is changed, in that one person leaves the stage rather than another, but such moments of truth will change the nature of victory or defeat.

Some scenes have become famous for this kind of duel between the actors: the Balcony Scene in *Romeo and Juliet*, the Quarrel Scene in *Julius Caesar* between Brutus and Cassius (this play has an unusually large number of contests, especially if the crowd of citizens is taken as one of the participants), the Nunnery and Closet Scenes in *Hamlet*, the encounters of Viola with Olivia and Orsino in *Twelfth Night* or of Rosalind with Orlando in *As You Like It*. The scenes between Macbeth and Lady Macbeth are comparatively short, but they contain many opportunities for subtle portrayals of acceptance and rejection. At their first meeting, immediately after Lady Macbeth has invoked the spirits 'that tend on mortal thoughts', the interactions start to work and shape each performance:

LADY MACBETH: . . . Come, thick night,
And pall thee in the dunnest smoke of hell,
That my keen knife see not the wound it makes,
Nor heaven peep through the blanket of the dark
To cry 'Hold, hold.'

Enter MACBETH.

> Great Glamis! Worthy Cawdor!
> Greater than both, by the all-hail hereafter!
> Thy letters have transported me beyond
> This ignorant present, and I feel now
> The future in the instant.

MACBETH: My dearest love,
> Duncan comes here to-night.

LADY MACBETH: And when goes hence?

MACBETH: Tomorrow, as he purposes.

LADY MACBETH: O, never
> Shall sun that morrow see!
> Your face, my thane, is as a book where men
> May read strange matters. To beguile the
>   time. . . .   (I. v. 47 ff.)

This brief episode can change many ways in effect. How do they greet each other physically? Do they embrace? When? How? Does Macbeth stop as he approaches his wife? Is he halted by his fear – the murder that is 'yet fantastical' – or because of his wife's elation and transformation? How far have the spirits 'unsexed' and possessed Lady Macbeth already, and is their power shown by quietness, hardness or ruthless speed? Does Lady Macbeth approach her husband, or wait for him? Does Macbeth close a door after his entry, and how soon and how deliberately? Is 'My dearest love' an attempt to find a greater intimacy or reassurance, and does 'Duncan comes here to-night' imply that Macbeth is reminding his wife of a pre-viously planned plot to kill the king? Or does the idea of murder surface into the words spoken only with Lady Macbeth's 'O, never shall sun that morrow see!'? Much will depend on how this line is uttered: does Lady Macbeth say it in order to strengthen her husband's resolve, or to share in a plan at which he has already hinted; or does she say the line for herself, without reference to Macbeth, as she assumes control over him and their joint destiny? Have they come closer together by now, and if so does Lady Macbeth walk away in the pause suggested by the short verse-line? Or does she approach him only now? In another enactment of the episode, Macbeth's single word 'Tomorrow' can be the fulcrum point in the contest between the two protagonists: it can be said firmly, as if refusing to murder, or it can be an avoidance of the implications of the question it answers; or, since the actor will have in mind his later 'Tomorrow, and tomorrow, and tomorrow' (V. v. 19) and several other echoes in Act III, it could show an early impulse to find some security beyond murder, to live beyond the moment of the killing – so it would be spoken as a kind of soliloquy from which his wife recalls him with more purposeful speech.

Much will depend on precisely how this first encounter is played, for according to its implications, its pauses, its changes of tempo, volume, pitch and rhythm and according to the stage movements, gestures, postures and facial expressions, the whole engagement between the two characters, the dramatic action will be set off to work out its own course. From this beginning, when they face each other to find trust and purpose, the actors will start a mutual exploration of the play, their characters and themselves, that will draw on all their conscious art and on their deepest beings. By the time of Lady Macbeth's sleep-walking and Macbeth's last soliloquies and desperate fight, the two performers will have found that all their resources have been called upon, and then *how* she moves off-stage with the simple words 'To bed, to bed, to bed' (V. i. 66) or *how* he finds the necessary physical energy for laying on to Macduff will speak wholly for them, bringing to the conclusion of the tragedy a response and expression that must be individual to each performer. The words, like the action, will now seem the inevitable culmination of each individual interpretation of the roles. Such effects can hardly be fore-ordained or prejudged; they involve the actor in discovery of hitherto untapped resources. Shakespeare's words can bear little of the dramatic burden alone, nor can they define the whole experience of the audience as it shares an unprecedented and thrilling illusion of reality. Essentially the last moments of Macbeth and Lady Macbeth are occasions for free and probing exploration, a shared and open encounter.

*   *   *

The very poetry of Shakespeare's plays which for some critics seems to provide a fixed point of reference, as if it were a bible to quote in unambiguous support of their own interpretation of a play, is for an actor an almost limitless collection of possibilities. Each speech offers thousands of invitations, even within regular metrical utterance. Meaning alters rapidly according to how loud or soft, quick or slow, high or low, the words are spoken; how they are phrased and pointed, what texture is given to the sound, what variation is introduced within a sentence or line, all change effectiveness and implication. The relative position of the characters on stage, their physical reactions, postures and bearing, the introduction of gestures or business and how these are accomplished, all interact with the words to create a precise dramatic effect which can never be wholly reproduced and in which verbal meaning is transcended by full dramatic action. The attention of the hearers also changes the implications of any speech.

Michel St. Denis described a dramatic text as a living organism. The actor is only the temporary mould that contains and limits its life-potential:

> You must be like a glove, open and flexible, but flat, and remaining flat at the beginning. Then by degrees the text, the imagination, the associations roused by the text penetrate you and bring you to life.

But it is each individual glove that speaks on the stage, nothing less complicated than that:

> the glove which is you, with your blood, with your nerves, with your breathing system, your voice. . . .[1]

This is an excellent way to describe the kind of life a text receives through individual rehearsal and performance. But such a description goes only part of the way towards accounting for the play in performance, when the words one actor speaks make their effects together with physical performance, gesture, stage-business and, above all, interaction with other characters and speeches, and when they are controlled by a developing

[1] *Theatre: the rediscovery of style* (1960), p. 69.

sense of what the whole play has become for each character in a particular performance before a particular audience.

Shakespeare's dramatic writing is both basis and suggestion for performance. It invites total co-operation, offering varying changes for each imaginative and resourceful performer to find his own voice and realization of his role. The co-operation must be active and explorative, involving a reaching out to the suggestions of the text and into oneself for the appropriate response. Often it is hard for an actor to know whether he is playing himself in Shakespeare's role or whether he has extended himself into another being. Unusual watchfulness is required to use the full potential of the text, to respond to the drama as it evolves between the various and contrasted characters and to be aware of opportunities for contrast, conflict and truthful innovation.

Shakespeare's writing for the theatre is essentially free. At a dinner-party, Vivien Leigh who had just played Viola and Lady Macbeth at Stratford-upon-Avon, said that one of the things that was scarcely realized about Shakespeare was how 'wonderful' he is to act:

> Shaw is like a train. One just speaks the words and sits in one's place. But Shakespeare is like bathing in the sea – one swims where one wants.[1]

This metaphor is, of course, double-edged, for in the sea it is possible to get lost or to prove too weak a swimmer.

A story that is probably apocryphal is told of Laurence Olivier in the role of Othello. The National Theatre production had been running for some time in London and to great acclaim, but one Thursday night, during the first half of the play, Olivier's performance seemed to grow in power and danger. Details that had been discovered in rehearsal and then lost, now reappeared. Some moments of silence became shorter and more intensely charged. Some vowels hung in the air, and some speeches seemed to be over almost before they had begun, as if representing the single breath of some instinctive and excep-

[1] Harold Nicolson, *Diaries and Letters*, *1945–62*, ed. N. Nicolson (1968), p. 297.

tional creature. During the interval the whole cast spoke in whispers in the green room, and when the performance resumed the spell still held. Other actors in the company topped their previous form and discovered the play afresh. Olivier continued triumphantly, risking more and gaining more than ever before. The applause at the end surpassed anything heard earlier in the run, but when Maggie Smith who was playing Desdemona looked round to congratulate Olivier, he had gone. She ran to his dressing room and as she opened the door her congratulations died before they could be spoken. Olivier was seated, looking as if he was in despair. 'Didn't you know how wonderful it was tonight?' she asked. 'Yes', came the reply, 'that's just it: I don't know why.'

Actors who perform Shakespeare can find themselves in an endless adventure, for ever finding new opportunities and new demands. Today they work in this way chiefly in rehearsals, for during the run of a production too frequent and too considerable modification of their performances would disturb the fix of the production and the confidence of their fellow actors. Besides, the freedom to re-interpret and discover is limited by the setting, costume, lights, sound and the many directorial decisions that have established a point of view and a single, clear interpretation for the play. The strongest evidence that actors can respond to Shakespeare's invitation for constant reappraisal and discovery comes from the days when productions were rudimentary and casting erratic and unstable. The *Journals* of William Charles Macready record something of the creative life of an actor who worked on single roles for most of a lifetime. They tell of both anxieties and excitements. In Birmingham on 13 April 1841 he recorded:

> Acted Macbeth with great spirit, i.e., began it so, and felt my acting begins to want spirit, which I must attend to. Was marred and utterly deprived of my effects by the 'support' of a Mr. —— and others in the last act. Was in a violent passion, and in that behaved very ill. . . .

But in Plymouth on April 26th following, Macready could record:

Acted Macbeth in my very best manner, positively improving several passages, but sustaining the character in a most satisfactory manner. . . . I have improved Macbeth.

He then went into details, such as:

The manner of executing the command to the witches, and the effect upon myself of their vanishing was justly hit off. I marked the cause. The energy was more slackened – the great secret. A novel effect I thought good, of restlessness and an uneasy effort to appear unembarrassed before Banquo, previous to the murder . . .[1]

Ten years later, in 1851, he played Macbeth for the last time, and he was still discovering the role:

Acted Macbeth as I never, never before acted it; with a reality, a vigour, a truth, a dignity that I never before threw into my delineation of this favourite character. I felt everything, everything I did, and of course the audience felt with me. I rose with the play, and the last scene was a real climax.[2]

Macready was an actor and not a writer, nor was he a man who could coolly assess himself, so these words tell little about the actual performances. But they are clear testimony to the actor's response to the endless opportunities of Shakespeare's text, even for a single performer. If his poetry is like a 'sea' for the actor to swim in, or like a living hand moving to fill an actor-glove, his poetry is also a mine full of unknown treasures, a personal, never-ending challenge to discovery and co-operation.

*   *   *

The corollary of this freedom and excitement is that Shakespeare's text is often difficult for both actors and readers. Its meaning seldom lies plain to sight and ear, and its implications and associations often build up in endless ramifications. Simple effects do occur in performance, but always the context and the preparation for them will not be simple.

[1] *Journals*, ed. J. C. Trewin (1967), pp. 171–2.
[2] Op. cit., p. 292.

When we consult the footnotes in modern editions of the play and follow their pursuit of Elizabethan meanings and the various implications of individual words as illustrated in Shakespeare's complete *Works*, we are inclined to think that the difficulty of his plays is peculiarly our own and the result of the changes time has brought in the use of language. This has, indeed, introduced new obscurities, but it has also eliminated others. Verbal usages which occurred for the first time in his plays – and the *Oxford English Dictionary* suggests that these were numerous – must have been unfamiliar and difficult to his contemporaries, whereas to us they are often part of common language, established there because Shakespeare has made them accepted. Elizabethan gallants took notebooks to *Romeo and Juliet* to garner new phrases for their own use – or so the story goes – and part of Shakespeare's intention seems to have been to stretch and excite the imaginations of his audience by new-coined words, unexpected associations, elaborate rhetoric and strained or eccentric syntax. There is a vigour and invention in his writing that cannot be followed by lazy actors or lazy audiences, and it will often be from passages that are only half-understood that a moment of shared clarity breaks with freshness and wonder. In this, as in their opportunities for actors, the plays court the unexpected and awaken expectation and individual imagination by a sense of contest and open-ended encounter.

As an example of how an audience can share an actor's discovery may be quoted William Hazlitt's account of Garrick kneeling as King Lear to curse his daughter:

> the first row in the pit stood up in order to see him better; the second row, not willing to lose the precious moments by remonstrating, stood up too; and so, by a tacit movement, the entire pit rose to hear the withering imprecation, while the whole passed in such cautious silence that you might have heard a pin drop.[1]

After such intense excitement and discovery, the applause could be tumultuous.

[1] *Works*, ed. P. P. Howe (1933), xxviii, 33.

Today applause usually waits for the stage lights to dim at the end of an Act, but in Shakespeare's day audiences were more obviously engaged in the unfolding drama. Shakespeare has Hamlet insist on the worth of a single 'judicious' critic, but this character is speaking in a special dramatic context and may not represent Shakespeare's own attitude to a 'whole theatre of others'. In *Richard II*, the attraction of a 'well-graced' actor is recognized as a fact of theatrical life. It was said of Burbage that 'he never went off the stage but with applause'[1] – not unlike many accounts of the applause that greeted Garrick in *King Lear*. In the Prologue to *If This Be Not a Good Play* (1610), Thomas Dekker described an audience as a crowd of vociferous 'fishwives' who roared their pleasure; but even they could be silent and on 'tip-toe' reach up to applaud with 'brawny hands' what their 'charmed soul scarce understands'. Elsewhere Dekker likened the audience's cries of approval to 'the breath of a great beast',[2] and Ben Jonson used exactly this image in commendatory verses for Fletcher's *Faithful Shepherdess*:

> ... the monster clapt his thousand hands,
> And drown'd the scene with his confused cry.

The audience of Shakespeare's day was undoubtedly stimulated by the excitement of a game or contest, and expressed their pleasure and sense of discovery by instantaneous applause whenever a performance achieved the unexpected or the exceptional. In the tragedy of *Barnavelt* (1619), the hero is likened to an actor:

> With such murmurs as glad spectators in a theatre grace their best Actors with, they ever heard him, when to have had a sight of him, was held a prosperous omen; when no eye gazed on him that was not filled with Admiration. (ll. 2475–82)

There are several accounts of plays being held up by applause, usually on the exit of an actor.[3] In their different ways, both

---

[1] R. Flecknoe, *Short Treatise of the English Stage* (1664).
[2] *Gull's Hornbook* (1609); ed. E. D. Pendry (1967), p. 98.
[3] See S. Harsnet, *Declaration* (1603), I2, and verses by John Webb prefixed to Beaumont and Fletcher, *Comedies and Tragedies* (1647).

Hamlet and Polonius illustrate this active response to words and feeling that, in the Elizabethan theatre, would interrupt, or mingle with, performance. Shakespeare's plays were written for this immediate, shared sense of discovery and achievement; they are open for exploration and endlessly varied realization.

6

An alternative Shakespeare

Current methods of producing Shakespeare's plays in the theatre flatly contradict the explorative and fluid engagement for which they were written. The director gives unity, the actors settle into their roles and the audience is kept in the dark to receive whatever view of the play has been chosen for them. Selected effects can be made powerfully, and excitement and expectation nicely controlled; and each successful production clearly and unmistakably re-interprets the play. Within this 'production' concept of presentation only small compromises can be made in the direction of freeing both the actors and audiences to create anew at each performance. Some major crises that involve only two or three actors can be rehearsed so that opposing forces are nicely balanced and able to respond to slight variations in performance from night to night. The production can be made more open to the 'feel of the house' by encouraging other actors besides the clowns to address the audience directly. Purposeful changes in movement or inter-pretation of character can be introduced during the run, parts exchanged, new actors brought into the company, the tempo of certain scenes altered, or lighting and costumes modified; in all these ways actors can be encouraged to remain explorative as far as the smooth running of the complicated production will allow. These are small changes, but together they can influence the performances and the reception of the plays.

In setting the plays some experiment is needed to ensure that the actor dominates the show-case, and not the other way around. Certainly too assertive décor should be avoided, and the handling of supernumaries and stage-business should not intrude upon the main drama that lies in the opposition of individual characters in action. Where theatres are not too large, performances might be given with the house-lights up, so that the audience can find its own point of focus in the stage-picture. But a broader, more outgoing acting-style would have to be developed to make this effective in even a small theatre of traditional design: the cost would be a loss of finesse that might be disastrous for Shakespeare's more mature plays. Our theatre-buildings, like our production methods, actor-training and audience expectations, work against the free and explorative performances that the plays naturally require.

Radical experiment is necessary to achieve a free Shakespeare performance. I would like to see what a company of about a dozen actors could achieve, if they were 'set upon a stage' and closely surrounded by their audience in the same light. The actors would have to be in charge of the whole enterprise, and its continuance should depend on their success. They would have few group rehearsals, sufficient only to arrange for the movement of supernumeraries and the handling of properties in the more elaborate scenes. They would be given their parts only, and not the text of the whole play, and most of the rehearsals would be in private study, or in twos and threes with no director to guide them. In group rehearsals and performance they would have the assistance of a book-keeper.

Undoubtedly at the start there would be huge difficulties, not least that of the actors having to gain confidence in this way of playing. Perhaps the best beginning would be for the actors to meet for only a few days of each week, while they were in another conventional production or while they were resting from other theatre work. A closely knit commune of actors working consistently on only one play would defeat much of the purpose of the experiment, for it is essential that each performance should be 'made' at the time of performance and should draw, at that moment, upon many diverse experiences. Even if a company grew up that could work exclusively in this free way, they should have at least a dozen plays ready for performance at any one time, so that they could benefit from the changing stimulus of the variety of their work. The actors should still rehearse mostly in private in their own homes, in contact with all other kinds of people and influences. They must have individual and independent lives, and must develop their own imaginations so that they bring a full experience to the service of the corporate and unprecedented fact of performance; in this way, they would continue to explore, discover and create. A theatre company that aims at 'free' performances of Shakespeare must not become exclusively theatrical and bound up only in itself.

The task of acting from a prepared knowledge and study of the text, and then improvising a response to the unfolding drama, would not be so wholly new to the actors as may seem at first. It is, in fact, a common experience during rehearsals in conventional theatres, whenever directors encourage actors to explore their roles. For example, Michael MacOwan has told how Granville-Barker used to keep his actors fresh during rehearsals:

> No sooner would an actor feel that he had settled into the mood of a scene, or a speech, and thought he saw smooth water ahead, than Barker would point out that a particular speech or sentence was outside that mood, that something new must be brought in . . . and every moment was to be made tinglingly alive.[1]

Actors often tell of the excitement of breaking new ground in rehearsal. For example, Peter Brook started rehearsals for the Mechanicals of *A Midsummer Night's Dream* in a separate hall and then introduced them, without preparation, to the courtiers, as John Kane who played Philostrate has explained:

> They had no idea of what was happening behind the studio doors and of course we had never seen before the play they now began to perform. They appeared as under-rehearsed as Bottom and his colleagues were in the text. Philip Locke as Peter Quince acted as the play's Prologue and its genuine prompter, holding the Penguin edition of the *Dream* in his hand. The court found this very funny at first, but as our jokes at their expense grew more desperate, the actual substance of their play together with the strangeness of our environment began to work upon us and by the time we had reached the death of Pyramus and Thisbe, their innocence had a weirdly moving effect on us . . .

[1] 'Working with a Genius', *Plays and Players*, July, 1954, p. 7.

We had many hours of black despair when we tried unsuccessfully to recapture the sensations we had first felt when we knew that a moment of the play had been 'experienced' properly.[1]

Peter Brook has branded as 'mediocre', the actor who is intent on using rehearsals to find a way of doing each part of his role and then to 'batten' it down, so that he is secure in his performance:

> The really creative actor reaches a different and far worse terror on the first night, . . . [He] will be most ready to discard the hardened shells of his work at the last rehearsal because here, with the first night approaching, a brilliant searchlight is cast on his creation, and he sees its pitiful inadequacy. The creative actor also longs to cling on to all he's found, he too wants at all costs to avoid the trauma of appearing in front of an audience naked and unprepared. But still this is exactly what he must do. He must destroy and abandon his results even if what he picks up seems almost the same.[2]

The excitement of newly created performances is a part of every actor's experience, and of those who watch them working in rehearsal. The free performances of Shakespeare that I am advocating would create conditions in which actors would find a retreat to fixed forms almost impossible. The audience would expect to watch for each new discovery, rather than sit back and allow a complicated and well-oiled machine to operate before them, a production in which what is new is almost invisible, if it is there at all.

Of course, Shakespeare's plays in this alternative theatre would not be formless or entirely free. Although unfixed by detailed rehearsal and direction, the drama would be held together by the structure of its action. In each play of Shakespeare's there is not only a plot but also a sequence in which full scenes with many actors on stage alternate in fixed order and proportion with more intimate scenes of soliloquy, duologue and interchanges between only a few characters. Moreover

1 'Plotting with Peter', *Flourish*, II. 7 (1971).
2 *The Empty Space* (1968), p. 115.

scenes are also alternately formal and informal, indoors and outdoors; they are variously political, religious, military, courtly or domestic; they are by day or by night, by winter or summer; they are of varying length and intensity. All these variations mean that in performance the drama has a fixed form of an almost musical quality that involves rhythm, proportion and shape. Such form is basic to Shakespeare's conception and it is often obscured in productions today. Only when the stage-business is not over elaborated by directors and designers, and when individual moments are not sustained beyond their natural length by carefully drilled responses, does this essential form hold all together and speak for Shakespeare in its own right in ways of which neither actors nor audience need be fully conscious. This form is necessarily effective in the unfolding performance through changes in grouping, in variations of movement, behaviour and bearing, in voices that change according to the kind of action portrayed, in the length of time between the natural breaks in the drama when the stage is clear or a halt in the action is unavoidable. All these effects complement or contrast with the interest of the play's exposition and narrative.

The drama would also be controlled in free performance by the text as it is spoken. As we have seen, the words change in implication and force from performance to performance, and variously reflect or contrast with the physical enactment, but the measure of the verse, the flow and interchange of the individual speeches and, especially in prose, the varying rhythms dependent on repetition and syntax, all provide fixed elements. In many modern productions this verbal form is obscured by the particular stresses that are carefully arranged to make specific points in each new interpretation, and exaggerated so that their effect is inescapable. Without the security of a fixed production, the actors would be more ready to use the flow and music of language to give their performance both authority and continuous interest. In a free performance the rest of the cast would not be drilled into silence and stillness to enable a speaker to sustain a pause beyond the time that the metre itself could sustain. With an audience sitting in the same light and open to many distractions, the 'spell', or music, of the verse and formal prose would be found to be a valuable and perhaps necessary means of holding attention.

But whatever form and attraction the play itself provided, this free Shakespeare would require that each of the twelve members of the company were skilled and experienced actors. They would need to be able to work creatively on their own. They would have to bring to performances a clear and unshakeable physical reality for each character, because only from such a base could the encounters of the drama be improvised with sufficient confidence and the opportunities of the text explored. They would have to be receptive to new influences and willing to question each achievement. They would have to be alert and adaptable, at once responsive to other actors and quick to see their own advantage. Once such a company was working, some training opportunities and some respite from major roles could be gained from playing the minor roles and supernumeraries which account for another dozen or so actors in most of Shakespeare's plays.

While the company should be given no director or producer or manager to take charge of the performances or their repertoire, there would be advantages in having someone to act for them in preparing the ground for each new play. But there should be no mistaking where authority lies, and such a person should be hired by the actors and be answerable to them; or he could be an actor who took less demanding roles and specialized in this important supporting work. His tasks might include research into the political and social background, the contemporary relevance and the stage-history of a particular play. He might suggest new interpretative possibilities to actors. He could provide details of appropriate rituals and ceremonies, for marriages, coronations, feasts, duelling, judgement scenes and so forth, from which the actors could make their own choice. He could edit the texts used for performances, prepare the book for the book-keeper and the individual parts for the actors. Possibly one member of the company would specialize in finding appropriate music for performances, another in arranging times and places for performances, another in co-ordinating finance. The company would have to find its own way of working and many different organizations would be practicable.

The most important features to insist upon are the primary control by the actors themselves and the ability to change from performance to performance.

The provision of costumes and stage properties might well be the responsibility of one member of the company who had special competence in this work and took lesser or fewer acting roles; or, again, someone could be especially hired by the actors for this purpose. In either case, the clothes worn on stage should be chosen in response to each actor's knowledge of his role and his enactment of it; they should be a response to the play as it came alive in private rehearsal and subsequent perform-ance, and they should be able to change as the performances change. In general, simplicity and expressiveness should be favoured, and clothes that are easy to move in so that actors are given free scope. Considerable problems will arise in responding to the periods of each play's composition, its setting in time and place, and the liveliness of performances for today's audiences. The right solutions will not be found by taking thought beforehand, but from the experience of working in free exploration and with the active co-operation of every performing member of the company. A start might be made by devising some uniform basic costumes to which each actor would add accessories, like hats, topcoats, swords or decorations to suit each part as he began to rehearse and perform it.

Although the actors would share the administrative tasks and reach decisions about repertory and finance by agreement, leaders would naturally arise from within the company. In acting, some few would set a dominant style, but these key men might change from play to play, or from one series of perform-ances to another. In order to let this kind of assurance evolve, a slow start to the venture must be insisted upon. From the first, however, someone would have to be made responsible for training and development. There are well-known exercises that would be useful in making the actors more able to respond to the challenges of this kind of performance, and so long as no group work was done on a text to be performed, a member of the company or a specially hired 'instructor' could take charge of training sessions without affecting the basic freedom of the performances. The actors' responsiveness to each other on stage could be developed by verbal and physical 'ring' games, where actors listen and observe closely in order to maintain a single line as each in turn takes over the speaking of a short speech or the enactment of some business. Exercise in movement and dance could develop the actors' expressiveness in space and time, so that they are more able to act as the designers of play on the simple stage and create three-dimensional moving groups of figures that express the dramatic event in the individual actor's presentation of character in action. Training in dance notation would encourage choreographic awareness and creativity. Some actors might benefit from exercises that could be devised to increase the quickness and scale of their physical expressiveness, so that small reactions discovered in performance would be simplified and enlarged, or extended from a part to the whole physique. Other actors would benefit from basic verbal work that taught how to respond to metre, syntax and figures of speech, and that increased their awareness of the text which is the backbone of all their work.[1]

Most important would be the provision of imaginative stimulus. In the work-rooms of the theatre documentary material relevant to the Elizabethan background and contemporary relevance of the plays could be displayed. Once a play had been performed several times, the actors might invite specialized criticism from other actors or persons especially interested in the particular play, its themes or stage-history. But in these matters, the most useful stimulus and instruction would come from the audiences whose free response will make an active contribution to the play each time it is performed.

*   *   *

As in all theatre work, the audience for this alternative Shakespeare is an essential ingredient, and one that must be right if

[1] Pioneering work must be undertaken to explore ways of using the basic 'music' of the text as a score for physical performance, so that the actors 'dance' in response to the words without losing the reflection of everyday behaviour which is necessary if the image of life on the stage is to remain close to natural behaviour and directly related to the experience of the audience.

the mixture is to work. The experiment should begin where a core of a few hundred interested spectators can be relied upon to come to successive performances. The studio work of some of the larger repertory companies already have such support and also theatres on university campuses. Possibly a Shakespeare Society, or group of enthusiasts, could act as sponsors, providing both the comparatively small initial finance and the core of an audience.

Free performances of Shakespeare would not have the obvious and indestructible attractions of regular productions as we already know them. But the plays would lie open for active exploration, for the audience to enter the enactment in imagination, and to discover for themselves those details that awaken belief and perception. Whenever this happens it is possible for the audience's understanding to reach out and, for the moment at least, include the whole play in a revelatory insight. If this happens frequently enough, the odds are that the actors will have won a permanent audience, for such creative participation has its own rewards that are effective far beyond the walls of the theatre in which the play is performed.

Ordinary concepts about what interests audiences should be suspect in this context. What is important is what happens in the minds of the spectators, not the splendour, clarity or obvious originality of what happens on the stage. Such imaginative response is likely to be more frequent when Shakespeare is performed than when the audience is watching an unknown play: the audience is able to supply part of the context for whatever detail catches their imagination. J. B. Priestley has recorded a common experience:

> More than once, at the end of a school summer term, I have sweltered at the back of the gymnasium and have listened to the lovely lines come piping out through cotton wool moustaches and beards, and have felt far closer to Shakespeare's heart and mind than I have done while attending some of the most elaborate professional productions.[1]

---

[1] *The Art of the Dramatist* (1957), pp. 78–9.

Such impressions in the minds of audiences are all the more possible when the actors finding their way into the play are experienced and gifted. Many times during rehearsals for regular productions, when the actors still wear their own clothes and a stool represents a throne, or two stools a bed, those who watch with attention can be transported with the performers; not only that scene but often the whole play and much else besides seems clear and immediately relevant. The loss of this power to transfigure when a complicated production is making its own points with irresistible effect is one of the discontents which may be counted on for starting the nucleus of an audience for an alternative and free Shakespeare.

The fragmentary and fugitive nature of the insights that a free performance might give is no disadvantage. Increasingly today we are suspicious of the artist who knows the answers to the world and makes his characters or his story explain everything as clearly as many directors would make their productions of Shakespeare. Many would understand why Edward Bond writes his plays so that they give a series of excitements, rather than a single, developing impression:

QUESTIONER: You were saying earlier, that you always write in brief episodes. . . .

BOND: The curious thing is that when I started to write I discovered I could only tell the truth in those short episodes and I felt those long scenes, those long developments aren't somehow true to my experience. I think they might have been true to Chekhov for instance . . . , and I can see, yes, that that's what life was like, that's the shape of life, that's the way it goes. But it seems to me that that's not the experience that one has of life now. It's much more, you see, full of contrasts and short things. . . . I wanted to say, look, it's happening.[1]

Each momentary, imaginative experience that comes from Shakespeare's plays in performance must of course be influenced by its context which includes the whole play, but in a

[1] 'A Discussion with Edward Bond', by I. Wardle and others, *Gambit*, v. 17 (1971), 28–29.

free presentation (which does not carry us forward all the time from one prepared effect to another) this more comprehensive response can make its effect at another level of consciousness than that which hooks us to the momentary revelation.

Shakespeare's words, too, would work on the audience by a kind of stealth. However new the perception of interplay between the characters, it would be held and partly defined by the words of the text, for words and sounds sometimes stay in the mind more clearly than the accompanying visual impression which first caught attention. The words are also able to help the audience to relate from the play outwards towards their own experience of life (and literature) where the same words are used and can become memorable. A free encounter with Shakespeare's plays will be both extended and contained by the words of the text, even while those words are being revalued and perhaps being made subordinate to a physical embodiment and a wordless excitement.

Much would depend on the closeness of the audience to the stage, for only at short range are the actors fully expressive without the simplifying and enlarging processes of a director's production (or without masks and a script intended for monumental performance as Shakespeare's plays are not). The actors should perform where no one is more than twenty-five or thirty feet from the stage. The nearer will be the better – even when this brings occasional blocking of one figure by another. When closely observed, every part of the stage reality – the groups of talking, living persons – is expressive in some way of the developing drama.

The absence of technical sophistication, in scenery, lighting and so forth, will mean that the actors could perform in any room of appropriate size, and this has important implications for audiences. Instead of productions geared precisely to the size and equipment of a particular theatre and not easily performed elsewhere, these performances would be essentially mobile and could seek out new audiences without greatly increasing costs. Only profit would follow a change theatre: the stimulus of a new audience's reactions and the alertness that the actors would find in working within a new stage-space and auditorium.

A comparison between our theatre methods and those of the Elizabethan theatre shows that we have never seen a Shakespeare play performed in a manner such as the author could have envisaged. We have seen only adaptations to another theatre-form which takes interest away from the individual actor who was the centre from which Shakespeare expected new dramatic life to spring in each new performance. Elizabethan performances cannot be reconstructed, but it would be possible to shift the focus back to ten or a dozen actors working freely and responsibly upon a stage. Such performances might be truly alive to contemporary thought and feeling, and awaken in their audiences a creative response in which imagination could find stimulus and extension. No one could guess what might be discovered in such a theatre, through Shakespeare's plays, and subsequently through other plays. This alternative Shakespeare could never rival the production of Shakespeare according to our present methods; it would aim at very different effects and probably it could never be widely popular. But the present monopoly needs challenging in order to recover some excitements that are now lost to public view, and to continue our exploration of Shakespeare's plays in new ways.

The theatre is at present seeking to define its own identity over against television and film, and any extension of its range will strengthen its self-knowledge in the unprecedented circumstances of today. Possibly the alternative way of staging Shakespeare, with its emphasis on immediacy and intimacy, might be peculiarly suitable to television cameras and so materially alter the financial prospects of all kinds of theatre work. On the other hand, the uniqueness of each 'free' performance, and the comparative cheapness of the enterprise, might encourage audiences away from television, which can reproduce only what is generally accessible.

The first task is to recruit a talented company and give them opportunity to work. For this kind of theatre they would need open and inventive minds as well as a wide range of theatre skills. I think these qualities would be found, for in our theatre productions and in the different arts of opera, film, music and ballet, Shakespeare's plays have attracted the best artists and not infrequently have called forth their best work. His plays seem unusually fecund, being not only imaginative themselves but also the cause of imaginative work in others.

*   *   *

I have put forward this alternative Shakespeare as a speculation because the practical experiments that I have already undertaken in this method of presentation do not provide the complete and continuous work which alone would provide the opportunity for a sound judgement on their achievements. Moreover the effectiveness of these experiments cannot be communicated by verbal description alone, since the talents and experience of the actors involved and the nature of the setting and occasion would all have to be explained, together with the essentially imaginative response of the audience. Perhaps it is no accident that accounts that have survived of Elizabethan performances of Shakespeare are so few, so fragmentary, and, for the most part, so dull: it seems likely that a free performance must always elude satisfactory description. The only undoubted fact about the effect of Elizabethan performances is their extraordinary popularity.

But my practical exploration has made some aspects of an alternative Shakespeare clear. For the most notable, I would borrow Brecht's word, 'spass': the play in performance becomes a kind of sport, or fun. This is obvious in the laughter which comes unheralded and unexpectedly, as sometimes it does in the rehearsal period of a conventional production. Such laughter is the overflow of a response that, while intent on the characters set upon the stage, is also able to have its own head. Such response is unexpected, innovative, energetic, and only rarely destructive. The audience seems to 'follow' the performers, and with them break into a new world: scales seem to have dropped from one's eyes, and everything appears new, gloriously funny, or clear and strong.

Besides laughter, I have known a dazed silence take possession of the room as Lear was reconciled with Cordelia; the audience seems to stop, as it were, with the actors and not a muscle moves. Such an intense and delicate attention is rare, and yet here it was offset by moments when the closely surrounded stage was so full that the drama seemed to break free of its bounds, repulsing complete or careful knowledge. Primarily this is an effect of contrast, for only some twenty people moving on stage in these performances can give an impression of crowding, noise and outburst when they enter to break down the audience's intense scrutiny of two or three figures. The effect is, I think, enhanced by the lack of careful drilling in group movement, so that there is indeed an element of jostling and restlessness even in a quiet scene like the funeral of Ophelia. When on a crowded stage, the actors do achieve a single, united response, or one speaker dominates by speech or action, the new clarity is the more powerful by seeming to be hardly won.

The loss of self-consciousness in the audience is remarkable, and I scarcely know how to account for it. Perhaps this happens only after a passage of boredom, or in some quiet moment before close contact has been created between actors and audience and while the performance is still cold and unadventurous. Perhaps the audience's freedom of response is simply a by-product of the unexpected, for no effect is certain in this kind of theatre and always the audience has a sense of discovering for itself.

7
Studying Shakespeare

Shakespeare, throughout the world, is both the most studied literary subject and the common factor in many people's acquaintance with literary culture. But during the last ten or twenty years there have been protests against the academic way with Shakespeare. Teachers, students, scholars and critics have all been arraigned for limiting the effectiveness of Shakespeare's plays by their own attempts to understand and explain.

Critics criticize themselves for clumsiness and inefficiency. Those who have pursued the meanings of Shakespeare's plays have warned that much has eluded their grasp, and that a recognition of 'pattern' is no substitute for an experience of the play. For example, Robert Ornstein's *The Moral Vision of Jacobean Tragedy* (1960) warns against its own approach:

> to attempt to define Hamlet's character by weighing his motives and actions against any system of Renaissance thought is to stage *Hamlet* morally without the Prince of Denmark, i.e., without the *felt impression* of Hamlet's moral nature which is created by poetic nuance. (p. 235)

And elsewhere:

> Only if we *surrender ourselves* to the moods of the individual plays – only if we enter as it were, the tragic universes in which the actions unfold – can we 'know' the ethics of the tragedies. (p. 46)

Wolfgang Clemen's study of *Richard III* does not attempt to define the ethics of the play or define its meanings. It is a 'Commentary' and not an interpretation:

> The author's aim has not been to present a book on Shakespeare to be read at one sitting, a new monograph presenting the play in a radically new light. . . . To ensure that we are scrutinizing

the text of a play with a sufficiently sharp eye, we must often change our perspective, looking first from one angle and then from another, applying at various levels the tools of analysis and comparison.[1]

Professor Clemen advocates mobility in an attempt to experience the play afresh and with open minds. While he has confidence in no single approach, he joins many other critics who have made a concerted effort to study Shakespeare's plays as in performance, so that the search for meaning is off-set by an exploration of those aspects of the drama that are not so readily reducible to verbal statement as theme, action or individual character. These critics, like Ornstein, seek to account for the 'felt impression' of the plays, studying visual effects, movements, groupings, rhythms, changes of focus, histrionic excitements, and so on.

During the last decade there has been a shift of position, but few academics wish to break free from a desire to explain, to find the secret, to reveal ever new meanings, to take into account further elements that are implied in a dramatic text. One of the earliest critics to attack himself and his fellows was Hardin Craig, in a lecture subsequently published in *Shakespeare Survey*, II (1949). He argued that Shakespeare was Pre-Cartesian, that Descartes's *Discourse of Method* published in 1636 had made us treat the dramatist as a specimen to be explained:

> Whether Shakespeare likes it or not, he must be compelled to mean something, must be subjected to research, explained by hypotheses, and demonstrated to the last detail.   (p. 108)

Craig believed there was little to be done: 'we must go forward, but with added care'. But he also asked a question:

> Shakespeare's art is large, multifarious, and relatively indefinite. It would follow that theses, to which our scientific method makes us habitually resort, do not normally arrive at these large effects and are not always conscious of them. They are not likely to do so as long as we pre-suppose or demand a modern kind of unity in Shakespeare. Can it be that Shakespeare had no one clearly

[1]   W. H. Clemen, *A Commentary on Shakespeare's 'Richard III'* (tr., 1968), p. xv.

definable thing to say about humanity when he put Hamlet on the stage, or that he did not mean some one thing by Coriolanus?

(pp. 113–4)

Craig and many other critics answer this problem by resorting to many approaches. Stanley Edgar Hyman for example has called for a 'pluralist criticism':

we can watch different critical vocabularies asking the question within their own system of terms, and getting an answer, not surprisingly, also within their own system of terms. In my view, putting these limited and partial – or overstated and reductive – answers together, on the theory of the symposium, that truth has a good chance to emerge out of the mutually corrective interplay of part-truth and error, one gets a richer sense of the critical problem – ultimately, of the literary work – than any single critical vocabulary or method can give.[1]

So in his book, Hyman places five different studies of Iago side by side, pursuing each for all it is worth and then saying little more:

I do not want to do my reader's work for him in putting together these five readings and allowing them to interplay.   (p. 138)

But some critics are now seeking for a substitute, an alternative 'study' that has little or nothing to do with a scientific simplification. In a paper called 'Meaning and Shakespeare', Norman Rabkin has called for a new beginning:

Shakespeare criticism is in trouble. One might not guess that from the ever-increasing rate at which it is produced, or from the obvious success its practitioners have had in reaching the goals they set for themselves, or from the substantial agreement on crucial plays and problems and methods. But a good deal of our agreement is based on a tacit understanding that the object of our search is the principle of a play's unity, that that principle is the play's meaning, and that meaning is therefore the umbrella under which we properly locate discussions of character, imagery, structure, dramaturgy, language, and intellectual and theatrical

---

[1] *Iago: Some Approaches to the Illusion of his Motivation* (1971), pp. 3–4.

history. We have learned how to do very well in such explorations, and I do not want to deny their unmistakable value. But I am going to argue that the better our criticism becomes, and the more sharply it is focused on explaining what plays are about, the further it gets from the actuality of our experience in responding to them, so that if we do not change our critical habits we are likely to betray Shakespeare as badly as did critics who wrote about the girlhood of his heroines.[1]

Norman Rabkin considered studies of *The Merchant of Venice* as examples of the 'trouble' in Shakespeare criticism, and easily demonstrated the contradictions and uneasiness which several of their authors betrayed when presenting their 'reading' of the play. He argued that it is as difficult to write about the meaning of a Shakespeare play as it is to talk about the meaning of an individual life:

> the decision no longer to be tied up in fruitless attempts to reduce significant process and teeming multiplicity to prosaic meaning is a liberating beginning, an invitation to examine the thing itself.
>
> (p. 104)

The implications of the word 'examine' in this call for a new beginning needs very careful exploration.

Perhaps it is not the right word, being still related to scientific particularity. The mainspring of our study should perhaps be an encounter, open, active, free and individual in the first steps. The sonnet by John Keats, 'On sitting down to read *King Lear* once again' speaks in terms of an imaginative and humble engagement:

> once again, the fierce dispute
> Betwixt damnation and impassion'd clay
> Must I burn through; once more humbly assay
> The bitter-sweet of this Shakespearian fruit.

Such openness to fresh impressions and such personal involvement will find meanings and contradictions in *King Lear* in plenty, but Keats's poem ends on a different note:

[1] Norman Rabkin, 'Meaning and Shakespeare', *Shakespeare 1971* (1972), p. 89.

> Let me not wander in a barren dream,
> But when I am consumèd in the fire
> Give me new Phoenix wings to fly at my desire.

For Keats, as for audiences in the theatre of his own day, Shakespeare's plays were open above all to ever-new creation: in the mind of this reader they called forth active and unprecedented response. Keats's poem is testimony to our freedom to enter the imaginative world of the play on our own terms and to find our own imagination kindled. Such an involvement is more important than any criticism, and is the necessary prerequisite and accompaniment for all study.

In my view, our study of Shakespeare has become too like our contemporary theatre practice. As we are given 'productions' which present the plays processed, developed and packaged according to a director's point of view and his actors' talents and predispositions, so we are given 'interpretations', new perspectives and various substitutes for the plays themselves. Has criticism and scholarship another role that will free the reader for active engagement?

*   *   *

The editors of the first Folio of Shakespeare's *Comedies, Histories and Tragedies*, his fellow actors and sharers in the King's Men, John Heminge and Henry Condell, introduced the book when it was published in 1623. They addressed themselves to a great variety of readers, 'from the most able, to him that can but spell':

> Well! It is now publique [they wrote], & you wil stand for your priviledges wee know: to read, and censure . . . how odde soever your braines be, or your wisdomes, make your licence the same, and spare not.

They said their function was not to praise the plays' author:

> It is yours that reade him. And there we hope, to your divers capacities, you will finde enough, both to draw, and hold you; for his wit can no more lie hid, then it could be lost. Reade him, therefore; and againe, and againe: And if then you doe not like

him, surely you are in some manifest danger, not to understand him. And so we leave you to other of his Friends, whom if you need, can bee your guides: if you need them not, you can leade your selves, and others. And such Readers we wish him.

The activity of the reader, howsoever odd his brain may be or his wisdom, is invoked by Heminge and Condell, and they obviously expect a hunt for an appreciation of Shakespeare's wit. Only after such 'licence' and variety of approach do they recommend the resort to other guides. Implicit in such a preface is a freedom of encounter not unlike that of the public play-house of Shakespeare's day where almost all ranks and conditions of men jostled to see and hear the plays; and to this reception the editors plainly refer when they continue and write of the plays' ability to stand their trial daily on the stage.

Times have changed, and now a reader has many more books and probably less time for any one of them, and he has no opportunity for seeing the plays 'stand trial' in such an open court. Today's reader of Shakespeare can purchase a book on each play, and in a single volume find many 'guides', all telling him how the play works as it is read or performed, and defining its central meaning, basic idea or contemporary relevance. It has become easier to join the critical debate than to experience the play freshly and imaginatively for oneself.

Some would say that we should leave such matters to the theatre and follow with analysis, comparison and learned exegesis only when the experience of the plays in performance calls for them. But to argue in this way is to be caught in a circle, for the plays we see in our theatres are very much the product of over-intellectualization and of a production-process that has much to do with highly sophisticated technical resources and our present economic and social structures, and works always to establish its own point of view. Perhaps if there were an alternative, free form of Shakespeare in performance, the active and questioning engagement of its audience would draw forth its appropriate scholarship and criticism. But for the most part, theatre experience provides corporate excitement and the stimulation of one particular interpretation, rather than an awakening of individual imagination and engagement.

Many readers will think they need no help. Instinctively they can enter the illusion of a play and realize all the physical, temporal and psychological implications of the text. But even these are limited by their own experience and energy of imagination, and could find further stimulation in seeing the plays in relation to other experience than their own: they cannot bring to their reading a whole theatre of reactions, in which they may share.

I think that for most readers the most obvious needs are to avoid being baffled by the absence of stage-directions and to overcome a habit of reading without visualization. Our education is almost wholly through words and it has become necessary to reawaken a sensual response, so that we see, hear and feel a play as we read, and entertain its many possibilities in terms of a living and ever-changing image of life. We must learn, too, how to take note of the musical element of a play, its rhythms, repetitions, tensions and relaxations, the signs of expectation, climax, anticlimax, transition and preparation. The plays have to become free and fully alive in performance in the theatre of the reader's mind.

Some books give aid here, considering how to read a text, what questions to ask in order to visualize what is happening on the stage. Editions of the plays can provide a theatrical commentary describing those effects of stage performance that are implied most surely by the text. But the danger here is that the reader's own response may be inhibited by a sense of competition with the editor. The enjoyment of a Shakespeare play can become a straining to see and hear what is said to be there, and to respond to everything. In these conditions it is hard for the free, outgoing imagination to become engaged.

Probably the most immediately effective way to encourage an appropriate engagement with the plays is to develop strategies for new modes of encounter. An experience of teaching can help here, for in a classroom it is easy to see when a student has become fully caught up in his study. I find one practical experiment useful as a beginning because it raises physical and visual problems in their simplest forms. No experience as actor, director or even playgoer is necessary for this approach to work. The reader provides himself with a board the shape of the platform stage familiar in reconstructions of the Globe Play-house, with entrances marked at the rear. It should be the correct size for pawns from a chess set to represent standing men. These pawns are then coloured, or marked in some way, so that each represents a different character in the play. (Toy soldiers or pieces from a game of Halma are easily available substitutes.) This is all the practical equipment needed – although there are obvious ways of making it more sophisticated – and the experiment begins by 'walking' the characters through the play. This sounds easy, but it is not: problems arise at once about the use of the two entry doors, the closeness of one figure to another, precedence on entry or exit, the timing of entries and (especially) exits, and so forth. But soon structural patterns become clear: the repetition of certain groups, the unusual nature of the movement in one particular scene, the complexity of one scene in comparison with its predecessors. One character is seen to be unusually isolated, others reveal themselves as particularly mobile or stationary; one character may repeatedly get forgotten, and so on. Moreover alternatives are constantly suggesting themselves. In my experience as a teacher, this experiment can awaken curiosity and imagination, and a zealous pursuit of solutions. An engagement which started very simply and with nothing more than practical common sense and a certain scepticism about the worth of the experiment, ends with many books studied in an attempt to discover the nature of Elizabethan theatres, the authority behind the stage-directions of the text, the meaning of particular words, the rank of a particular character. Many solutions are attempted and a grasp of the dramatic action gained which leaves the student endlessly curious because his invention, if not his imagination, has been awakened. A free, unlimited, three-dimensional exploration of the text has started.

Only certain minds will be caught in this way, and there are many other simple practical engagements that can be tried, some being more effective with one reader than others. What, in my view, is essential at the beginning is to by-pass a purely verbal response and evoke living images. In a class I have given three or four students the same sets of photographs of six different actors in the role of Iago. I ask them to take the pictures away and arrange them in order of preference, and then come back to defend their choice at the next meeting of the class. Again this exercise needs a willingness to be elementary, but this is only at the beginning. Once students try to justify one face rather than another, and to argue with someone who has chosen another photograph, they become involved in the text and its suggestions of human reality. From the text they refer to their own knowledge of human beings, and what they defend is their own response to the text in theatrical terms: again, this classroom exercise is not as simple as it seems. A variation is to ask a class to cast a play from actors they know on film or television; this is the beginnings of creating their own performance of the play in the theatre of their minds. Again the exercise leads back to scholarship, criticism, the minutiae of the text, and life and thought in Shakespeare's England and in our own world. The same basic task can be started more simply still, by asking individual members of a class to choose colours for the costume of each character in the play, or to describe what modern clothes would best suit the individual characters. All these exercises work best when several students are given the same tasks to work at separately and then come together to discuss their choices and try to arrive at an agreed scheme for the whole play; in this way something of the varying possibilities of the text may be realized. Better than a classroom atmosphere is that of a game, with its freer interplay of fantasy and discovery, and a positive desire to know the other players' minds.

It has long been recognized that group participation is a useful way of stimulating exploration. The simplest form of this is a class reading. This may be fine for the gifted actor who is given the lion's share, but an embarrassment or unrelieved boredom for many other students. Moreover it does little or nothing to realize the visual and physical elements of the play. Many schools and universities go further and make a practice of staging Shakespeare's plays in public performance, so that pupils, teachers and scholars may have first-hand experience of rehearsals where the text is explored practically and of performance where the play is seen to come alive and find its new shape, weight and speed in action. Professor Clifford Leech has said that every Shakespeare scholar and critic should have had the experience of acting in the plays.[1] But such methods are costly in time and money; and they can do harm.

An educational stage production has grave difficulties: the demands on time, effort and money are obvious, and beyond those are a wide range of technical problems that have little to do with an imaginative response to the play and require specialized knowledge of lighting, painting, costuming and organization. The impossibility of all students getting commensurate benefit will be recognized from the beginning, and the tendency of the gifted actor to take the whole operation as an indulgence in what he can easily achieve is not the least of the later problems. Such productions are valuable for exploring the dramatic qualities of Shakespeare's plays, but they are so only for a very few of the students involved. Those who start with the greatest interest can become obsessed before long, not with the play, but with their own inability to perform in the way that they have come to see that they should. Acting, especially in Shakespeare's plays, is not as easy as it can sometimes look: educational productions are complicated group exercises that make huge physical and psychological demands. Only a very wise teacher-director can keep a balance between aspiration and achievement, and only a few of those involved will learn as much about Shakespeare as they do about themselves as actors and about the difficulties of theatre production without adequate training, facilities or time. Alternatively, the student actors can be protected from criticism and come away from the experience thinking that they have effected wonders and be more pleased with themselves than excited by Shakespeare's play.

Some teachers have turned from the ardours of play production and substituted the provision of films, video-tapes and sound recordings so that students can see and hear a wide range of alternative renderings of a scene or of a whole play. They use these to start discussion among their students and indeed they do provide something like a serve-yourself theatre experience. But the experiment is without true audience contact with

[1] At the 1972 Shakespeare Conference, Stratford-upon-Avon; 'The Incredible in Jacobean Tragedy', *Shakespeare Survey*, 26 (1973).

the play and without the physical reality of stage and performers, and it escapes from the excitement of real time.
Moreover the cameras have shown the audience where to look
and how to look. The viewer is more passive, and his range of
vision greatly limited. Even rapid experience of these wholly
different productions of a single play seems to work against
a true exploration of Shakespeare: they are seen so close
together in time and are so wholly different in concept and
filming procedures, that the large differences of presentation
tend to leap to attention rather than the similarities or the
variety implicit in a single intense moment. Attention is often
drawn to acting and filming techniques which are not subjects
that can be appreciated or discussed responsibly without a great
deal of specialized knowledge.

   All these means of experiencing Shakespeare's plays in performance have been used to advantage and, together with
ordinary theatre going, they provide the basis of many students'
and scholars' appreciation of the 'felt impression' of the plays.
But simpler means are available. Shakespeare's imaginative
range and fertility, and the free form of presentation for which
he wrote, combine to make even a short passage from a play
capable of awakening a recognition of the drama's endless life
and suggestiveness. With a tape-recorder a solitary student can
begin to explore the text in sound. He must first be simple, and
taking some six or seven lines from a soliloquy or public speech
record them first loudly and then quietly, then slowly and then
fast, in high pitch followed by low, followed by varying pitch.
He should choose one word in each line to stress particularly,
and then vary the stresses; and then choose two or three stresses
in each line. He should then pay attention to metre, and record
the same passage with the iambics marked with pedantic
regularity, and then less strictly. He should speak in long
phrases and then in short; take breath at different points, and
so forth. As he is engaged in these recordings he should stop
from time to time to play back and so begin the process of
choice and rejection. Which seems right? What is the effect
of this rendering, and then of this? Which seems most suited
to character, sense of reality, musical interest, which seems
most suited to the play as a whole. All this time he has changed

his reading of the lines merely by changing the manner of speaking them. Instead of seeking to express his own under-standing of character or of the meaning of the lines, he has been entirely fluid in his rendering. The advantage is that this random sample of interpretations will have suggested new meanings, implications and effects which he would never have foreseen for himself. The longer and more varied the merely technical experiment continues, the more suggestion will be received back from the tape-recorder. In my experience, this experiment works with almost everyone who tries it and is prepared to be a little simple in speaking and listening. The pace of work soon quickens as the reader gains more variety of reading and is quicker to reject the material that proves to be without interest to him.

Of course, for exploring longer speeches, duologues and more complicated interchanges between characters, more than one reader is almost essential, and in a classroom or game situation, a small audience can replace the tape-recorder with great advantage in immediate registering of effect and a quicker recognition of what is happening. The next development is to work on the same scene, introducing various uses of space and movement, and later of gesture and bearing. All this should be effected without calling on anyone's powers as an actor: indeed the tendency to perform should be gently inhibited at first, so that one or two participants do not run away with the game and so that everyone remains fully mobile in their readings and movement and able to respond objectively to what occurs. The object of the experiment is to awaken suggestions of how the scene might go, not to create a dramatic rendering. The decision to start acting may come later, when everyone is ready and some few 'interpretations' are ready for a final test of credibility. But at this point the experiment will be over.

For early experiments short episodes should be chosen where only a few characters are involved. Scenes with obvious 'ful-crum' lines are particularly useful, for they offer widest scope to varying interpretation. For example, when exploring *Hamlet* a sequence of such scenes could be explored so that attention centred on lines like:

I shall in all my best obey you, madam.

> I will watch to-night;
> Perchance 'twill walk again.

I do not know, my lord, what I should think.

O all you host of heaven! O earth! What else?
And shall I couple hell?

You cannot, sir, take from me anything that I will more
willingly part withal – except my life, except my life,
except my life.

I did love you once. . . . I loved you not.
I was the more deceived.

Now, mother, what's the matter?

How is it with you, lady?
> Alas, how is't with you?

I loved Ophelia.

The rest is silence.

These procedures are simple and they need time and patience
if they are to work. They can help participants to become aware
of the fluid elements of acting and staging, one by one, so that
the effect of each may register. The slower and simpler the
work is done, the more various and more revealing will it
become. The sooner, too, will individual participants be ready
to continue such experimental, theatrical reading for themselves, awakening slowly and variously a whole play to life in
the theatre of their minds, beginning in fantasy to enact and
realize more of its roles and scenes, in ever-changing possibilities.

There are various other practical exercises that help towards
a full presentation of the play in the mind. One is to try to cut
a text by as much as four or five hundred lines, justifying each
of the excisions. Another is to try to visualize each physical
activity required by a chosen passage of the text, enact them
in mime or reality and then try to speak the accompanying
words. Listening to appropriate music and choosing which to
use in a production, deciding on costumes and properties and

dances – any problem is useful that makes one consider a physical and aural stage reality, because it extends response beyond the words' purely literary and personal connotations. A student who undertakes this exploration will be involved in many basic reappraisals as the play reshapes and reforms itself in performance in his mind.

Such an exploration of a play avoids the full demands that Shakespeare makes on individual actors; it is lightweight and all too flexible. But while it misses that depth of involvement which an actor achieves and which the plays draw upon so marvellously, it does prepare for an appreciation of the actor's art and the excitement of actual performance. It is a foundation for further study because the 'thing itself' has been encountered free of intellectual conceptions, something has registered of its 'felt impression' and its changing 'moods'. Student, scholar, critic and teacher all have equal status in such experimental readings, for all will be aware that the meaning of a line cannot be pinned down, still less the effect of the meeting of two characters in a moment of intense feeling, or of the stage full of named and un-named characters. If our study of Shakespeare is on the right lines, these experiments will have no conclusion.

If the study of Shakespeare is based on dramatic exploration, more than the imagination is awakened. To be involved in the plays' imagined world is to discover many questions: what kind of queen was Cleopatra, who was Isis, did Desdemona give Othello a 'world of sighs' or a 'world of kisses', does Hamlet enter now or then, what is a fool, how does a man die, what does 'I love' mean and what 'I want?' In my experience, the student who is most imaginatively involved in Shakespeare's plays learns to think quickly and read widely, and he makes judgements. (By the way, he does better in examinations than his teachers have expected.) He knows Shakespeare's words, and treasures and studies them and many of their implications, because they are the food of his imaginative and real life. He is constantly responding to the plays anew, in freedom and with growing responsibility and ability. For him, the plays are opportunities for encounter, not puzzles that must be made to yield clear answers.

*　　　*　　　*

This account of 'free Shakespeare' has ended with a description of a pedagogic exercise. For some readers, this will seem remote from their own instinctive enjoyment of Shakespeare, either in the theatre or in reading. But the exercise is not described as a necessary approach for everyone; it is a suitable conclusion for my book because it presents the kind of response I believe Shakespeare's plays require in most elementary and dismembered form.

My whole argument is that we should postpone judgement in favour of open-ended exploration, that only when our minds are filled with images of men in action have we begun to realize the wealth of Shakespeare's imagination. The texts of the plays can feed the closest and most precise scrutiny, and they can activate creativity in us all.

8

Free Shakespeare

Throughout this book I have argued against a processed experience of Shakespeare's plays. The packages are useful, stimulating and, often, carefully and expertly prepared, and I would not be deprived of them either as a playgoer or as a reader and student. But they are nowhere near as necessary for me as an encounter with the plays themselves, preferably in free performance by actors of talent and originality.

Above all I would like to see performances of an actors' company that had dispensed with the ways of working and thinking that lead to a 'production'. I would like them to forget the very word and, with it, 'designer', 'director', and all those elements of theatre work that are involved with long-running, permanent successes. They would work for the sake of performances, each modified by its occasion and audience, and by their own developing imagination, understanding and skill.

'Sit in a full theatre', wrote John Webster, the dramatist, 'and you will think you see so many lines drawn from the circumference of so many ears, while the Actor is the centre.'[1] I wish I could sit in a theatre of such endless originality. The evidence of theatre history is unequivocal: in Shakespeare's day, and for hundreds of years afterwards, a close, almost exclusive attention to the actors sustained enjoyment and discovery. The originality did not spring from some new mode of staging or some new dominant theme, but was the result of an exploration of Shakespeare's plays by actors who lived with his roles and modified their performances from night to night, and acted with giant imagination and resource for a free audience. The director, trying to reinterpret a play, is most sure of his effect when it does not depend on the continuing reality of a created character; he is most in control when he plunges us in sudden

[1] 'An Excellent Actor', *Characters* (1615).

darkness, sets all the characters a-giggling, fills the stage with totems, trapezes, mirrors, music, dancing, plastics or abracadabra. In contrast to this, a free, actor-centred theatre would provide an encounter with Shakespeare's plays at which everything was at risk, and from their prepared positions the actors, with the audience, could probe, penetrate and ride high upon the plays in their moment-by-moment life. In place of theatrical tricks and organized clarity, we might discover a kingdom on the stage – various and human, often divided against itself, and yet capable of order, wealth, honesty and health. The actors might be princes – powerful and independent in their own rights, mindful of their lineage and their responsibilities. And the audience might act as if they were monarchs. The metaphor, of course, is Shakespeare's, from the Chorus of *Henry V*, and in other ages than our own it was applicable to performances of his plays. The men set upon a stage are sufficient mirror to hold up to our lives, so that in its image we may find the form and the pressure of our age.

But historical precedent is not necessary for my argument. Every time an actor tells me of a discovery that was made in rehearsal and yet was hardly discernible in the finished production, I know that the plays could live freely upon our stages. When silence grips a rehearsal room, or whenever one is in the presence of an artist working at risk, whenever one joins others instinctively in genuine celebration, and whenever one reads Shakespeare's plays and a new image arises in one's mind of how, for that moment, the play could be, at all these times I am sure that for me there is a simpler, more open, active, exploratory and free kind of Shakespeare in performance than any production that I have seen.

As a student, I would like to forget 'argument', 'criticism' and 'interpretation', in favour of exploration and encounter. I would like to learn how best to experience the plays as images of human action and to respond creatively to their great wealth of suggestion. I do not wish to pin down the plays, but allow them to take wing in the freedom of my own reactions, so that they enlarge and refine my imagination. This is not to invoke mindlessness, but to set one's attention upon a living, moving target. From such an exploration criticism and judgement are bound to arise in their own time. Only the questions will be different, involved with what the plays do in particular encounters, not with what they always are. The centre of critical attention will be an engagement with the plays in their theatrical context, as they take infinitely varied life on the stage and in the minds of the participating audience.

I believe that actors and audiences need a release from the pressures of commercial success and sure-fire effects, and that students need to explore images of life as they know it, rather than seek the 'meaning' of a play. Liberation is necessary, and the patience, responsibility and imagination to take advantage of it.

9

Changing Shakespeare, 1996

When *Free Shakespeare* was first published in 1974 it seemed to be saying what many others in the theatre were on the point of saying. Directors had realised that each new production could not pretend to wrest a meaning out of the text which no one else had seen before. Peter Brook had already taken his Stratford *Midsummer Night's Dream* to an entirely new environment in Birmingham for one night only, in order to free the actors and allow them, on that occasion, to take possession of the play and their audience. Soon after the book's publication, a "Free Shakespeare" production of *King Lear* arrived at the Edinburgh Fringe Festival and a "Free Shakespeare Company" established itself in Chicago. In London, in 1974, Mike Alfreds had started Shared Experience, a company working on non-dramatic texts by co-ordinating the actors' improvisations (*The Arabian Nights, Bleak House,* etc.) and some years later they tackled their first Shakespeare, *The Merchant of Venice*. A group of actors took a joint initiative and founded the Bremen Shakespeare Company in which they performed all the usual roles of directors and producers, as well as performing in the plays. A little later in the nineteen-eighties, Cheek by Jowl would establish itself as a touring company in Britain and around the world, using sparely designed settings and playing what their publicity was to call a "regeneration game, the fruition of impulses from a collective creative imagination." Shakespeare's plays became the most constant element in their repertoire and reviewers recognized a new and restorative approach:

> the company tries to lay the text and the action open to public scrutiny. They aim at an emotional continuity between actors and audience and a fresh accessibility which gives fire to the dry tinder of the text.[1]

[1] Quotations from Simon Reade, *Cheek by Jowl: Ten Years of Celebration* (London; Absolute Classics, 1991), pp. 10-1.2

In *Free Shakespeare*, I had called for performances to be staged in spaces where the audience sat around within some thirty feet of the acting area. While conceding that such proximity to the actors would involve frequent blocking of sightlines, I argued in favour of the greater effectiveness given to the interplay between persons on stage when seen at close range, the larger contribution under these conditions of physical responses, tensions, signs of imbalance, of the very breath of life and drama. All these advantages came to be used regularly in the later seventies and eighties, even by companies that had the resources for mounting far grander productions. Buzz Goodbody's production of *Hamlet* in the intimate Other Place theatre of the Royal Shakespeare Company — even smaller than the size I had envisioned — appeared in the same year as *Free Shakespeare*, in 1974. This initiative was followed by notable RSC productions of *Macbeth*, *King John*, *Titus Andronicus*, *Othello*, and other Shakespeare plays, all cast with senior actors and directed by the company's Artistic Director as well as by younger newcomers. By the nineties, intimate Shakespeare had become an established form of staging, valued on an equal footing with productions on far larger stages and for audiences ten times the size.

Over subsequent years, many of the directors whose work had been described in my book, began to change the way in which they spoke of their tasks. By 1993 Peter Hall, for example, would insist that neither the director nor the actors knew what their work would discover: "to start out rehearsing with a concept which is imposed inhibits creation and prevents discovery."[2] For *Antony and Cleopatra* in 1987, he allowed himself "the luxury of an especially long rehearsal period" and so was able to leave the design to the last moment:

> Normally, sets have to be designed well before rehearsals start. This time . . . Alison Chitty's work was able to evolve organically, the usually unattainable ideal. For the first three weeks Alison sat with us and sketched furiously while we discovered the physical dynamic of each scene. Only then did she design it.[3]

[2]   *Making an Exhibition of Myself* (London; Sinclair-Stevenson, 1993), p. 83.
[3]   *Op. cit.*, p. 341.

In rehearsal, if not in performance, a younger generation of directors values the inspiration of a moment more highly than any earlier concept or pre-determined interpretation; for example, Anne Bogart writes:

> When things start to fall apart in rehearsal, the possibility of creation exists. What we have planned before, what we have in our mind in that moment is not interesting. Rollo May wrote that all artists and scientists, when they are doing their best work, feel as though they are not doing the creating, they feel as though they are being spoken through. How do we get out of our own way in rehearsal?[4]

A movement towards a greater respect for the momentary inspiration of actors, or of directors when working closely and watchfully with actors, is found throughout theatre in the later nineteen-nineties. Dramatist and director, David Mamet, has argued against all the complications of staging which theatre attempts when it tries to compete with film or to enforce a particular reading on the actors:

> Broadway theater by no means withstanding, the best production is the least production. The best production takes place in the mind of the beholder.
>
> We, as audience, are much better off with a sign that says A BLASTED HEATH, than with all the brilliant cinematography in the world.[5]

He sees a malaise in theatre that began with the director's growing power over actors:

> This paternalistic pattern in the theater infantilizes the actors, so they feel compelled to please rather than to create, to rebel rather than to explore, to perform rather than to express.[6]

Another development of the nineteen-seventies and eighties which would have been surprising only a few years earlier, was the provision of public "workshops" on Shakespeare's texts. Audiences are drawn to watch as actors encounter the problems of acting the characters as if for the first time. Often that is just what is happening and the same scene will then be repeated several times in different manners, suggested either by

4   Anne Bogart: *Viewpoints*, ed. Michael Bigelow Dixon and Joel A. Smith (Lyme, New Hampshire; Smith and Kraus, 1995), p. 10.
5   *A Whore's Profession: Notes and Essays* (London, Boston; Faber and Faber, 1994), p.119.
6   *Op. cit.*, p. 130.

the actors or by someone conducting their open-ended exploration of a text. These unpremeditated performances may be given in a theatre without a set on its stage, or with one from whatever production happens to be playing at the time. They may also be given in school and college halls which the actors have entered for the first time only minutes earlier. Sometimes workshops will continue over a number of days and can evoke a response that is perhaps more lasting than that given to the most "finished" production. A few actors from the Royal Shakespeare Company, who became known as A.I.R. or Actors in Residence, would spend weeks at a time interacting with students at North American universities in exploratory workshops and also performing freely staged, abbreviated versions of the plays. For actors these initiatives provide opportunities to develop their own individual approaches to the texts and to particular roles; they also encourage an exceptionally open style of performance that is capable of lively interplay with audiences. Several series of Shakespeare workshops have been made for television; one of eight programmes for the Open University and BBC 2 has been screened regularly for fourteen years after it was first recorded and has been sold for transmission around the world.[7]

While the early seventies had seen a movement away from too much directorial control in rehearsal, too reductive "interpretations" for each new production, too restrictive and headstrong stage designs, too large auditoriums, and stages too remote from an audience and too reliant on pictorial effect, in the nineties the effects of other confinements have become more evident and threaten to reverse these other liberating tendencies. The most obvious changes are due to the development of all aspects of theatre technology and design, spurred on by the rapid advances of film, television and videos, and by the success of spectacular "mega-musicals". The arrival of these new resources for staging Shakespeare was heralded by the appearance in the "credits" for each production of a "Sound Designer" alongside those for set, costumes, and lighting. This func-

7   The workshops led by John Barton for a Channel 4 (London Weekend Television) series have been recorded in a book, *Playing Shakespeare* (London and New York; Methuen,1985); however these are not typical of the form, the RSC director playing a more interrogatory and presentational role than usual.

tionary, unknown in the nineteen-sixties, had become a prime player in the making of a production as early as the end of the seventies, together with the lighting and set designers. The combined effect of computers, infinitely variable lighting, and multi-channeled, highly sensitive sound was still further increased with the use of self-propelled and remote-controlled scenic units. Together with the actors' performances, audiences receive re-arranged and overwhelming sense-experiences. By these means the impact of a production can be nicely judged, precisely repeated, and certain in effect.

Descriptions of two scenes from Terry Hands' production of *Coriolanus* which toured Europe at the end of the nineteen-seventies show how these new effects are applied:

Scene 2 (Act One, scene two)

Drums and a stereo double rattle effect accompanied the sudden strong side-lighting of a bas-relief upstage — a triptych: two black-velvet gold-studded figures in follow-spots facing inward to a central golden-headed warrior powerfully lit in powerful stance. These still figures, the Volsces, "Tullus Aufidius with Senators of Corioles", spoke, in a strong echo-effect, of their preparations to meet the three roman war-leaders and other forces.

Scene 29 (Act Five, scene six)

[Alan] Howard's entry [as Coriolanus] from the far back wall, to tremendous martial music from the whole brass and full light, follow-spots tracking him step by step down stage, was given high power by the moving of the greater and the lesser walls each side, together, to make a new, and extraordinarily powerful, stage-shape, so that Howard seemed to enter between two black cliffs. Precisely at the climax of the music he placed his sword before his feet on the ground, centre-stage.[8]

Music was "live" in this production, but already the sound designer's work was evident in the echoes and enhancements that worked together with all the other mechanised and computer-controlled effects. The results achieved, according to this account, were 'powerful, strong, tremendous, full, high': repeatedly, they are said to give 'power' to the drama.

By the nineties, computers and complex sound systems were within the means of even very small companies. Whereas

[8] David Daniell, *'Coriolanus' in Europe* (London; Athlone Press, 1980), pp. 24, 40.

the cost of sets and costumes had risen astronomically because they cannot be mass-produced, the provision of complicated micro-equipment for light boards and sound consoles had benefitted from the competitive prices of a hugely expanded market and mass-production techniques. Today almost any theatre company can afford to create a subtle and emotive "soundscape" and hundreds of immediately effective changes in the intensity, direction, and colour of light, all of which is able to establish, fill out, and repeat with absolute certainty a series of effects that capture an audience's attention. A few actors alone are hard pressed to enter into competition with such powerful means of expression that speak directly to the audience's senses. They would need the greatest skill and considerable time in rehearsal, and then work at a great disadvantage. An operator can flick from one light-effect to another in a pre-arranged moment or in a controlled sequence of imperceptible changes, so that a general impression of danger, or formality, or isolation, or (again) power has amazing impact. "Now could I drink hot blood", Hamlet will say and the very earth can actually seem to quake and the air above him darken, before he has any need to say anything more. The simplest single word can be enough to hold attention, no matter how it is spoken, when an entire world upon the stage seems to hold its breath as it is spoken, or lightens or presses down upon the speaker.

Actors are no longer free to move and speak on stage. They must remain carefully within the pre-set technical trickery that makes their performances eloquent or emotive beyond their own capacities; if they do not, anything they can do may be rendered ineffective. By following exactly the timing and movements that have been arranged for them by director, designers, and technicians, "powerful" effects will be assured. An entire production can be made impressive and secure. In the late nineteen-sixties, actors could not have been confined to this extent and a Shakespeare play in performance would have been, naturally enough, much more free.

A moment's reflection will show that while directors have talked about the actors' freedom and their unique responsibility as creative artists, these same directors still remain in charge because what they position around the actors has become hugely more impressive. Companies, such as the Actors' Company in Britain and the Bremen Shakespeare Company in

Germany, which were founded in the name of actors' autonomy, have either gone out of business or have given their chosen directors a power and their productions a style that are not very dissimilar from those found in the larger established theatres against which these actors had rebelled. Technological advance has called for a number of operators to "run" a production and these key players remain outside the stage-action where the life of the drama used to be concentrated and from which any definition or excellence used to be solely derived. To take command of the technicians and operators and tell them what to do, the director was already in place and, by doing this, his or her hand has been greatly strengthened.

Financial pressures have also confined performances of Shakespeare's plays. In common with other arts at the economically straightened end of the twentieth century, theatre needs to satisfy its accountants at every turn and this constraint affects every aspect of work upon the stage. More particularly, successful productions must be exploited financially by being repeated again and again at the time when the people who have created them need, for their own artistic reasons, to move on to new work and new risks. Even the smaller and leaner companies, such as Cheek by Jowl, have succumbed to the promotional demands of the marketplace and given up the "fresh accessibility" which comes from staging a number of productions in quick succession. Their actors are now engaged for extended tours of a single production which will often last a whole year or more, or will settle into a London theatre for months at a time. These arrangements give financial stability to the company and help to establish a "bankable" name-awareness that will ensure future work, but they condemn the actors to all the dangers of routine repetition.

In well-established, building-based theatre companies, financial restraints ensure that patterns of work are calculated so that they use the least possible time and money. The season's repertoire, the programming of construction and rehearsals, the hiring of guest directors and designers, the marketing of product, and so on are all designed with an eye to economy. Such a tight hand limits a production's freedom to explore and develop, and its director's ability to respond to the actors' discoveries. Operating under these conditions, John Jory, Producing Director of Kentucky's Actors Theatre of Louisville, has declared himself in favour of directors who know what they want at the start of rehearsals. He sees a strong concept as the essential means of unifying a production in the time that is available:

> The geniuses of our age can rely on and delight in spontaneously profound insight; the rest of us need to plan. Coming into rehearsal without thematic ideas is like setting out for Boise without a road map. Whenever directors describe their intentions as "finding the play in rehearsal," they don't.[9]

Most theatres which have to satisfy subscribers with a succession of fully-staged productions have developed a routine of work in which output, impact, and consumer convenience are more important than innovation or discovery.

A different organization is needed for theatre, one that provides for a repertoire of plays, frequently changing and responsive to local, topical, and personal influences; a production schedule in which the actors' creativity sets the pace, shape, and emphasis for every other element; an administrative structure which gives to actors the possibility of personal development and a release from the tyranny of long runs or extensive tours of a single play. Theatre needs to shake itself out of patterns of work, methods of finance and cost-control, and means of production that were all developed years ago when its resources were very different and its potential audiences were living very different lives with very different expectations.

These changes need to go along with a style of rehearsal and staging which harnesses the new technology to the actors, and not the other way round. A contact between actors and audience must be achieved that gives immediate access in both directions and the closest possible view of the intricate and yet sometimes very simple interplay between the persons of the drama. The issue is not that of a puritanical and self-inflicted poverty of means versus a great richness of effect; nor simply that of the power of directors over against that of actors. The problems involve every means of control and freedom on stage, the management of scale and focus, use of repetition and innovation, and the organization and finance of the entire operation. All this needs to be reconsidered in facing the particular demands of staging Shakespeare's plays in a new technological age. It may be that the challenge of producing these plays will lead theatre forward in other operations as well.

9   "Why Directors Can't Direct," *American Theatre* (October, 1996), p.7.

For students of Shakespeare's plays, a new edition of *Free Shakespeare* is also timely. The nineteen-seventies had witnessed a shift away from accepted modes of criticism and scholarship and, for a time, freedom was in the air. *Alternative Shakespeares*, a collection of essays published in 1985 (London; Routledge), paraded samples of new "approaches" or methods of study: semiotic, post-structural, feminist, Marxist. Eleven years later appeared *Alternative Shakespeares 2* which featured psychoanalysis, sexual and gender politics, race, and new historicism as tools of the critical trade. Many anthologies and book-length studies now list or exemplify a host of new recipes and recommend one after another as procedures to follow in order to respond responsibly and more fully to the plays. Instead of a free encounter with the texts, bringing personal experience and topical and local interests to bear, a critic or scholar has been given patterns of study which serve to "privilege" this reaction or that. In a confusing world, such guidance is attractive. It is reassuring to follow in the footsteps of acknowledged leaders and to have a method that seems to guarantee a reward. An effort to listen to instructions may, however, leave little time for reading the plays with that freedom of mind that respects their many possibilities of enactment and brings irreplaceable personal experience to bear on the imaginative task. Unprogrammed reactions may be lost and adventurous considerations obscured while Shakespeare's plays become reconstituted under one or more of the many brand names. Multiplicity has had the effect of narrowing a student's gaze. Great advances in scholarship and criticism have been due to the increased awareness of methods of proceeding and yet, re-entering this continuing debate, a new edition of *Free Shakespeare* may usefully remind its readers of the rewards of a free, personal, and imaginative engagement with the details of the texts; a rapidly changing society calls for no less.